Spooky Origami

Marc Kirschenbaum

Fit to Print Publishing, Inc.
New York, New York

Spooky Origami

Copyright © 2020
Fit To Print Publishing, Inc.

All rights reserved. No part of this publication may be reproduced, stored in a retrieval system or transmitted in any form or by any means, electronic, mechanical, photocopying, recording or otherwise, without the permission of the copyright holder.

ISBN 978-1-951146-09-2 (Paperback Edition)
ISBN 978-1-951146-10-8 (Hardcover Edition)

The diagrams in this book were produced with Macromedia's Freehand, and image processing was done with Adobe Photoshop. The Backtalk family of typefaces was used for the body text and the cover uses Haunted with PT Sans. Ellen Cohen assisted with the cover design and provided valuable artistic assistance.

Contents

Introduction	5
Symbols and Terminology	6
Skull with Bow	10
Ghost	14
Black Cat	18
Bat	22
Jack-o'-lantern	26
Spider	31
Alien	36
Witch	42
Grim Reaper	52
Japanese Monster	61
Hand in the Box	69
Dracula	82
Skeleton	95
Materials and Methods	111
Paper Sizes	121

Introduction

People love spooky things to get their adrenaline going or just to satisfy some morbid curiosity. Having something scary tempered with some cuteness allows us to peer a bit closer to our demons. Origami is the perfect art form to recreate our favorite monsters and other sinister things - its angular forms dilute the frightening elements to make them more palatable. Japan especially has infused adorable elements into even the most ghoulish of creatures. It is therefore fitting to utilize the Japanese art of folding paper for these models.

Macabre icons have even been exploited for commercial potential. A few of the pieces are loosely based on attention-grabbing scary icons. This includes the super-simple *Ghost* and the very detailed *Japanese Monster*. There is even an entire franchise based around the included *Skull with Bow*.

Death and the occult are popular subjects, so models of a *Witch*, *Dracula*, and *Grim Reaper* are showcased. These figures capture our imagination of what could be in the world beyond. Moving just a little bit closer to reality, the included *Alien* encapsulates our fascination with the unexplored universe beyond.

No collection of spooky origami would be complete without some representations of skulls and bones. The *Skeleton* model showcases the full set of bones, while the *Hand in the Box* takes a whimsical look at the expressive extremity. Just because something exists naturally does not mean it cannot invoke fear. Accordingly, models of a *Bat*, *Black Cat*, *Spider* and *Jack-o'-lantern* round out this collection.

All these pieces follow the one square no cuts philosophy. This makes for some interesting and sometimes challenging folding sequences. These origami models are arranged by their approximate level of difficulty, so you can work your way up to the harder ones. Naturally, there are thirteen projects included to provide many hours of folding fun – apologies to those suffering from triskaidekaphobia. Enjoy!

Symbols and Terminology

Line Styles

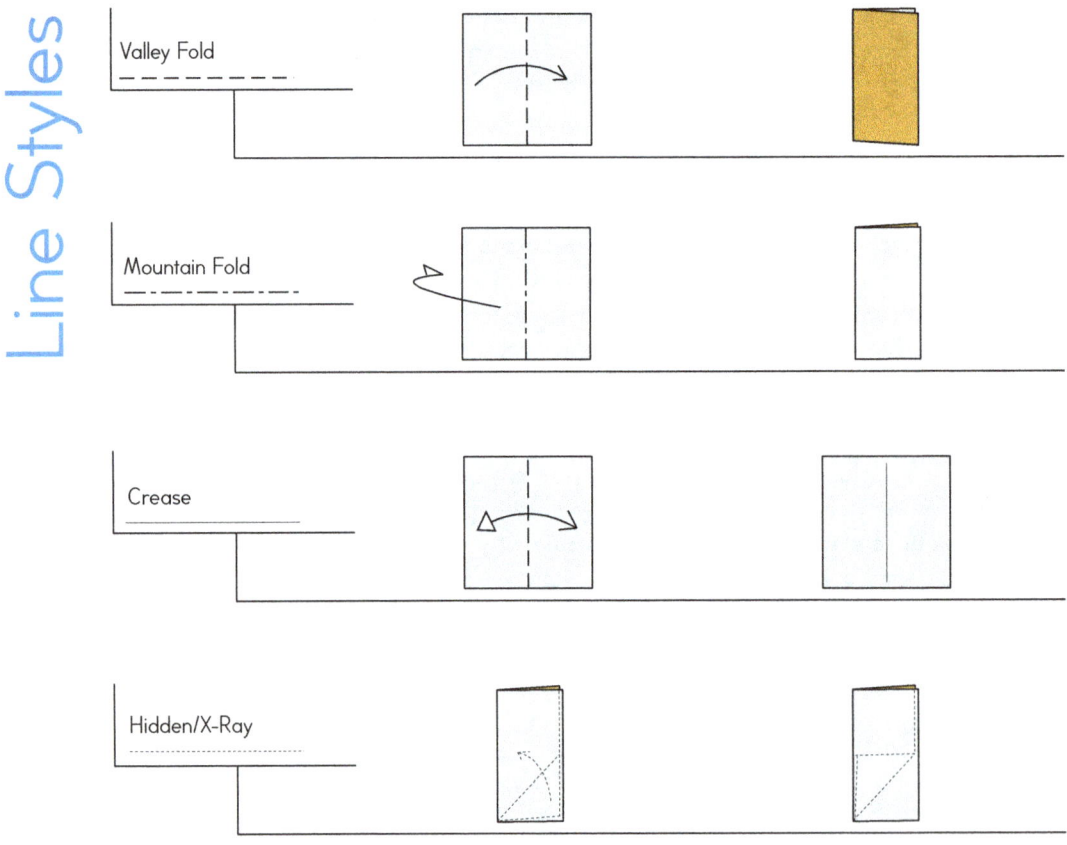

Valley Fold

Mountain Fold

Crease

Hidden/X-Ray

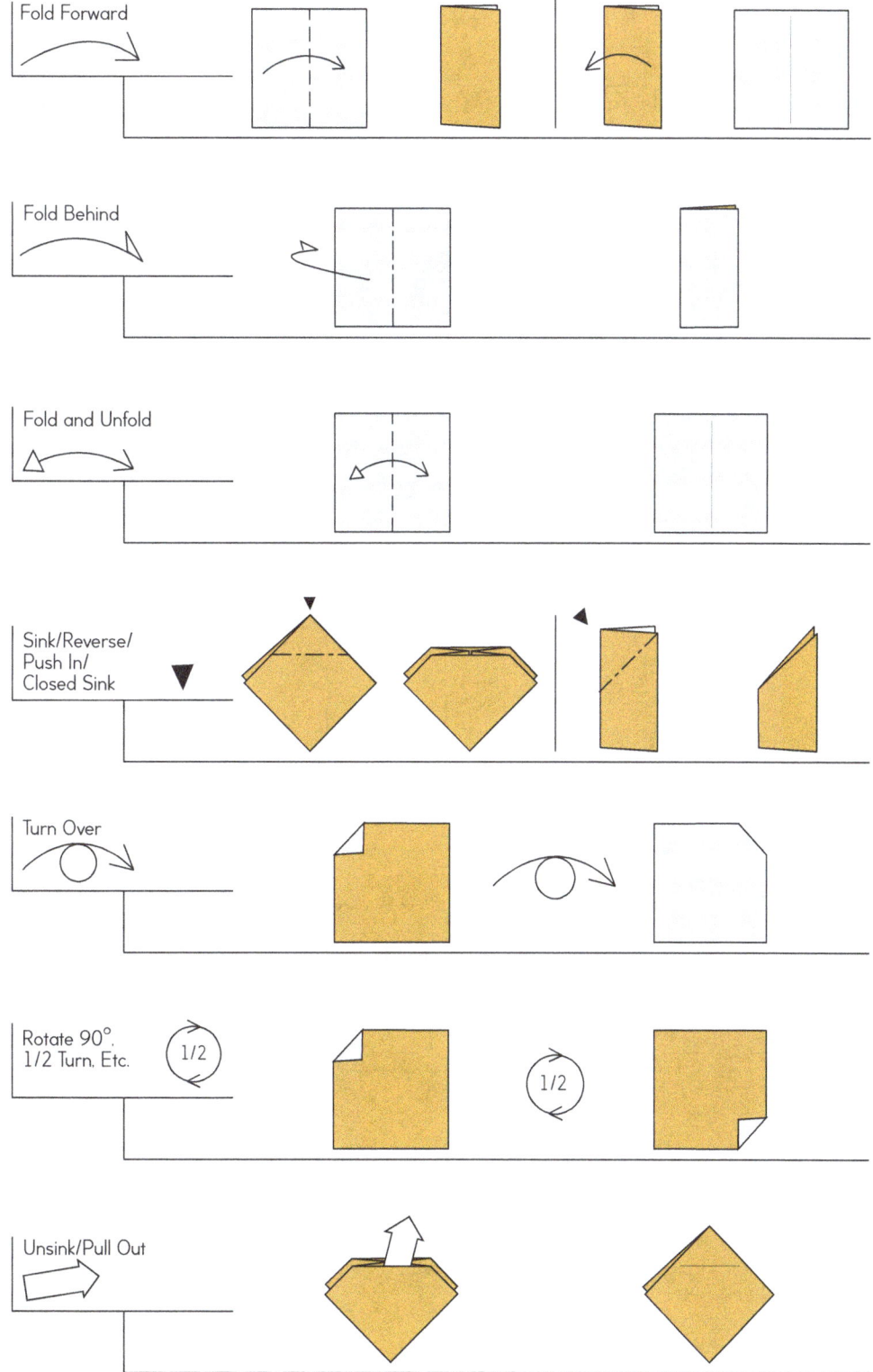

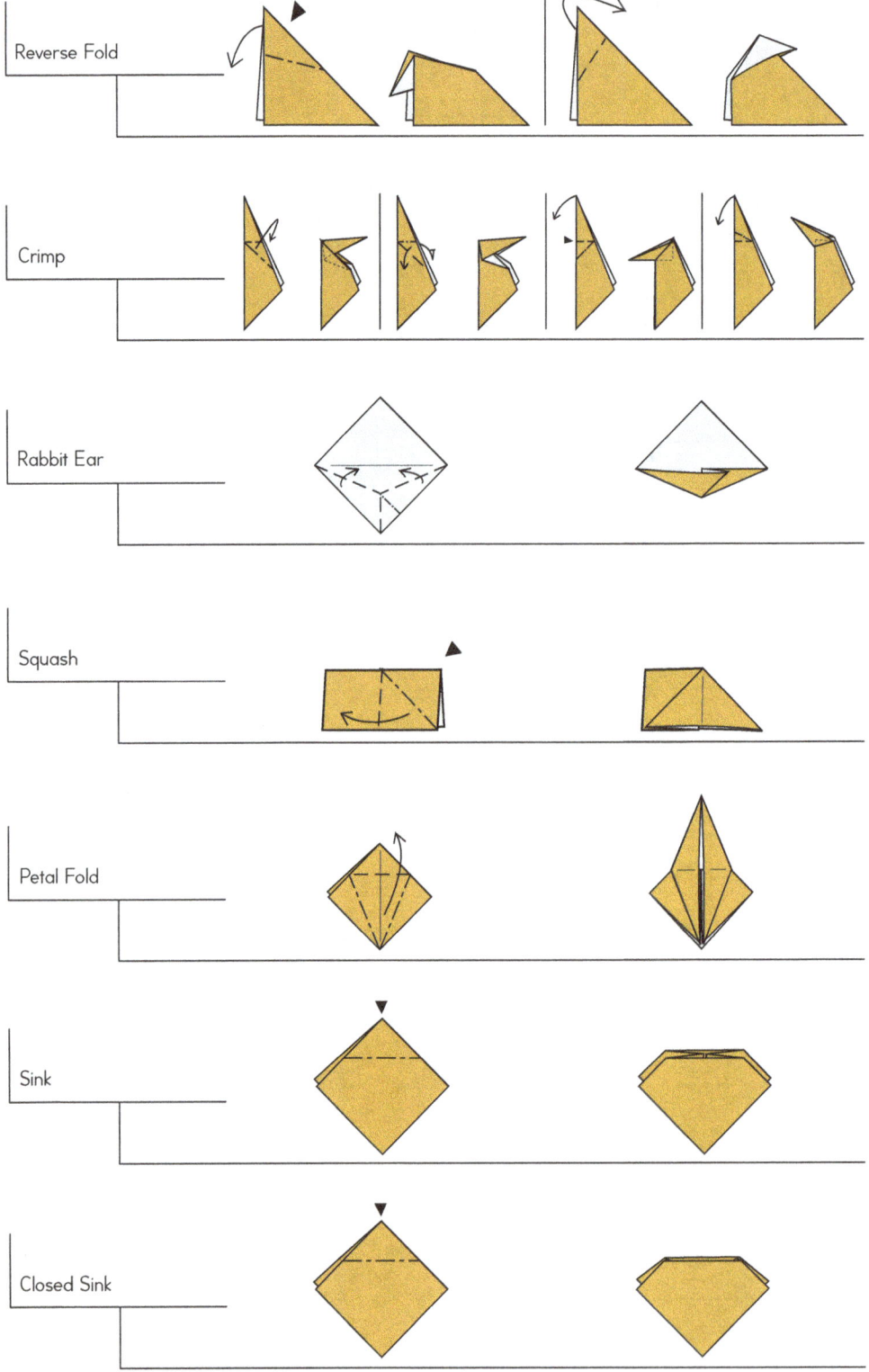

Sink Triangularly

Pleat

Swivel

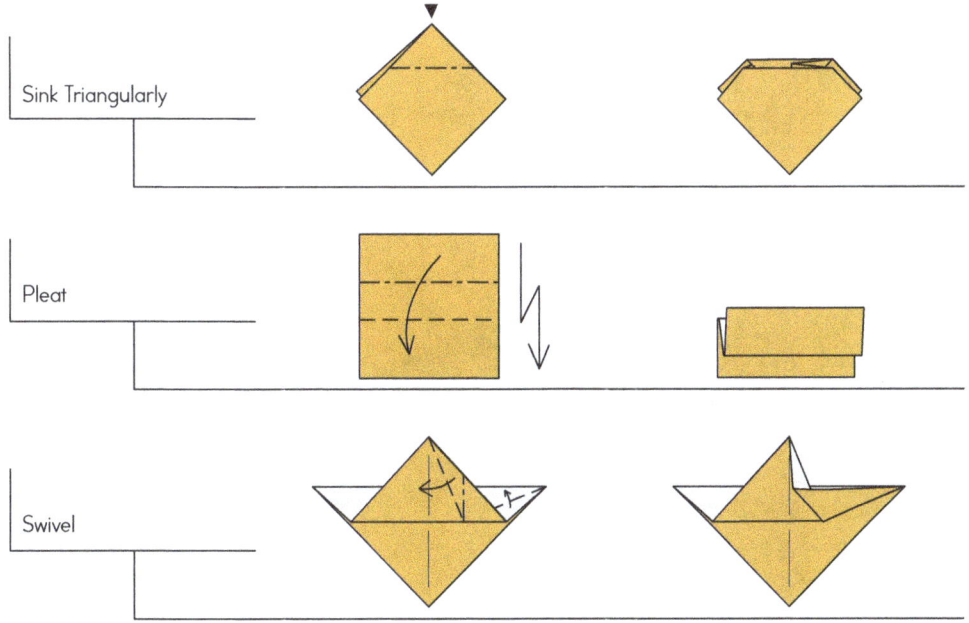

Skull with Bow

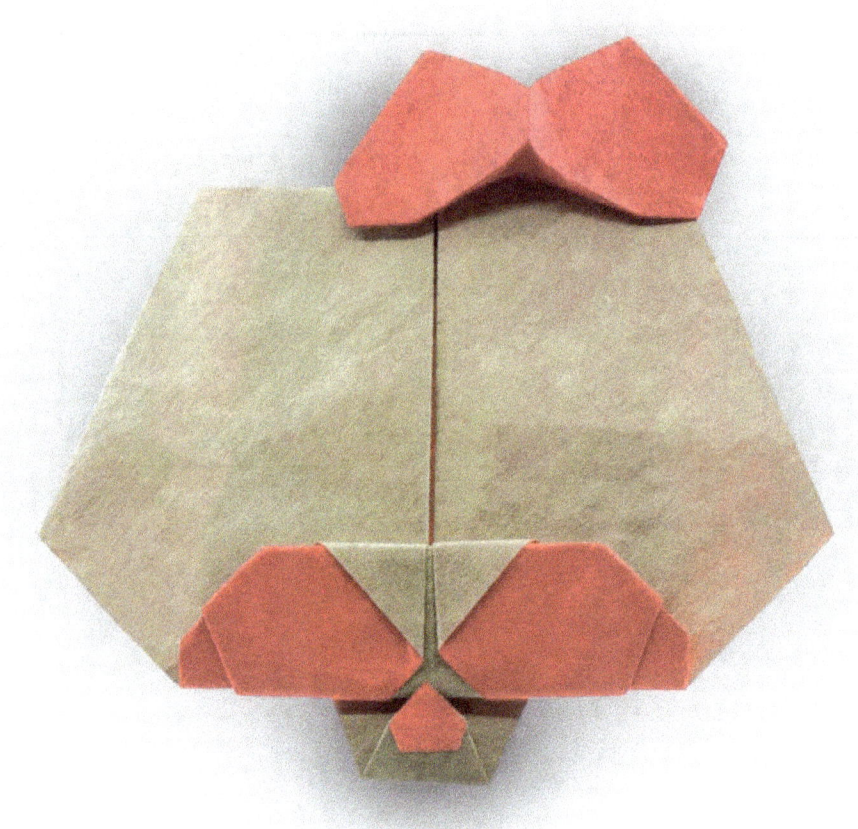

Merging a bare cranium with a bowtie is the epitome of a spooky-cute hybrid. This brilliant idea came from a major toy company that has been targeting cute versions of famous monsters towards young adults in the form of books, toys and movies. Observant folders will notice that only simple valley folds and mountain folds are utilized for this origami version of a *Skull with Bow*. This style was coined *Pureland* by British folder John Smith, a perfect point of entry for newer folders.

skull with bow

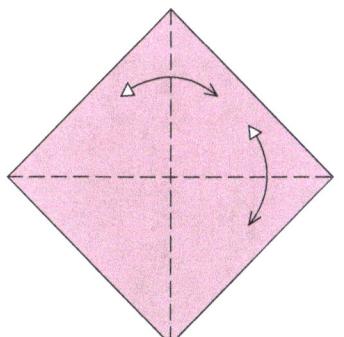

1. Precrease in half along the diagonals.

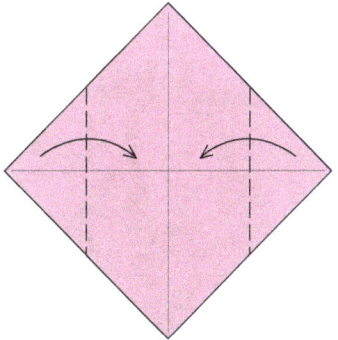

2. Valley fold the corners to the center.

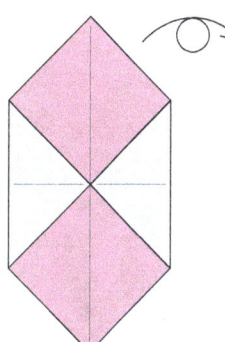

3. Turn over.

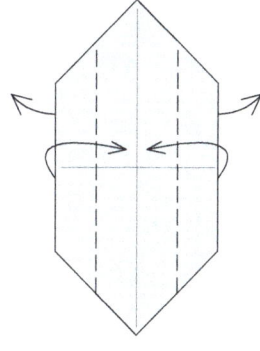

4. Valley fold the sides to the center, allowing the flaps from behind to flip forward.

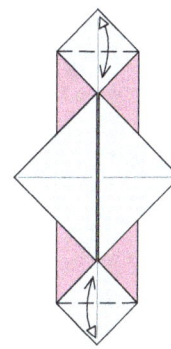

5. Lightly precrease at the top and bottom.

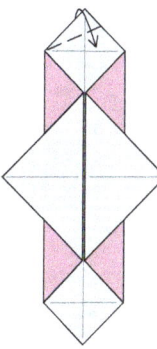

6. Valley fold to the top crease.

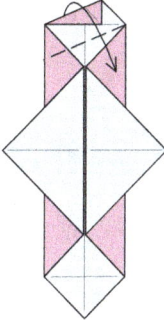

7. Valley fold so the edge hits the side.

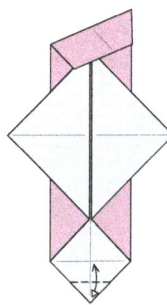

8. Lightly precrease towards the bottom crease.

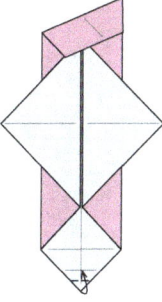

9. Valley fold towards the last crease.

11

skull with bow

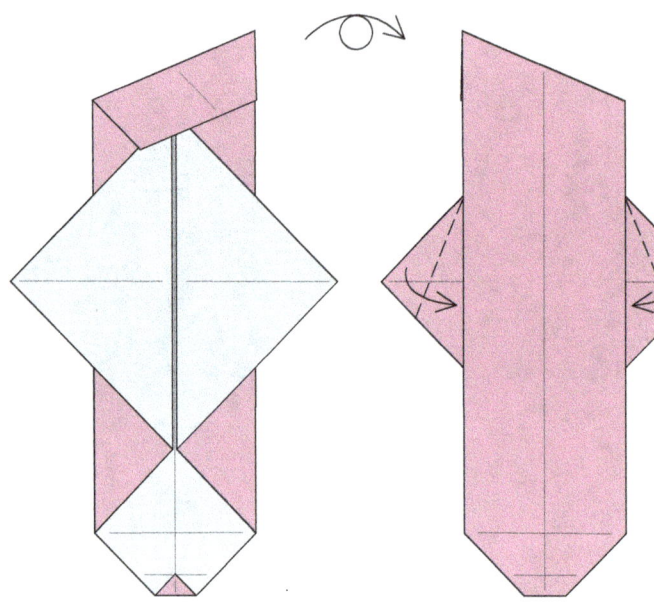

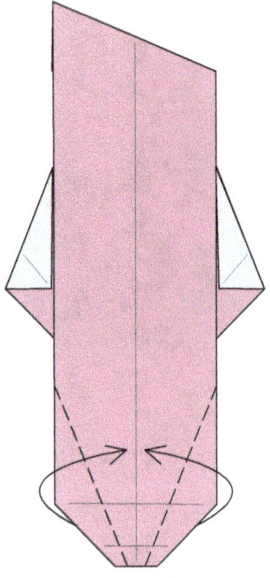

10. Turn over.

11. Valley fold towards the folded edges.

12. Valley fold along the angle bisectors.

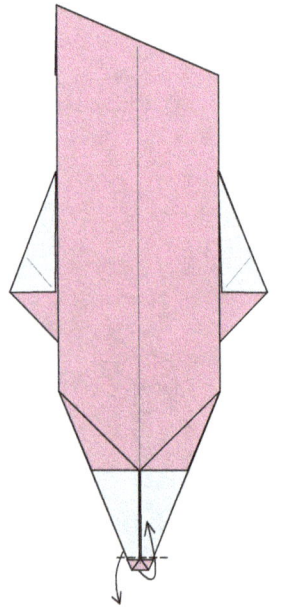
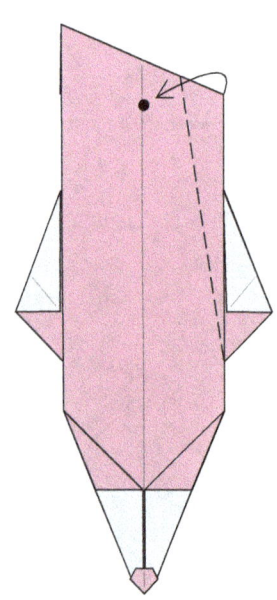
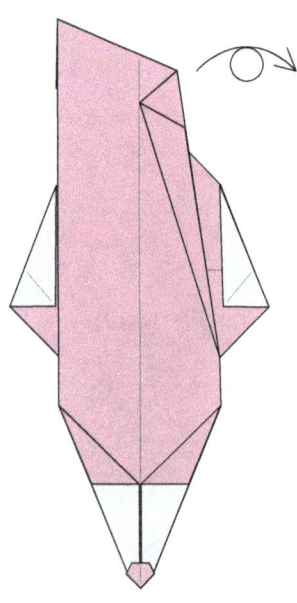

13. Valley fold, allowing the flap from behind to flip forward.

14. Valley fold towards the center crease.

15. Turn over.

skull with bow

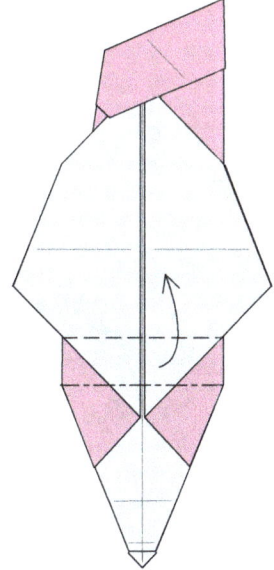

16. Pleat the flap up.

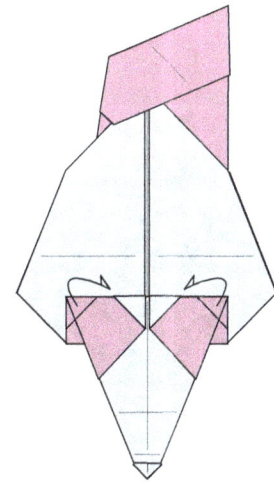

17. Mountain fold the corners.

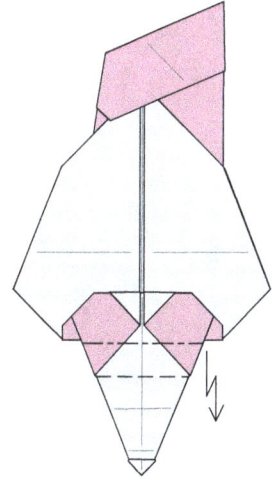

18. Pleat the flap behind.

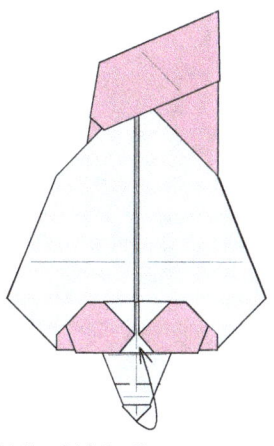

19. Valley fold the flap up.

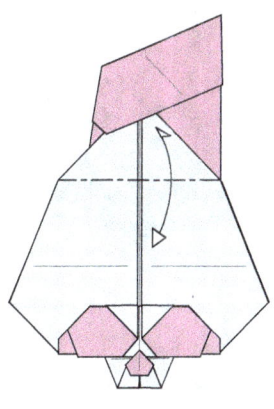

20. Precrease with a mountain fold.

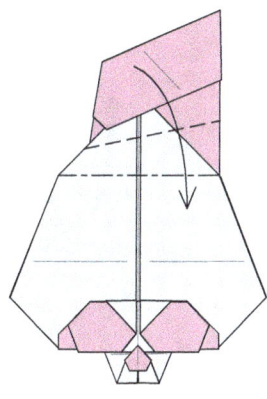

21. Pleat the flap down, allowing the bottom edge to wrap around the top of the skull.

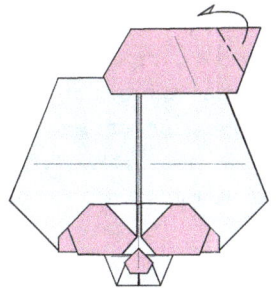

22. Mountain fold.

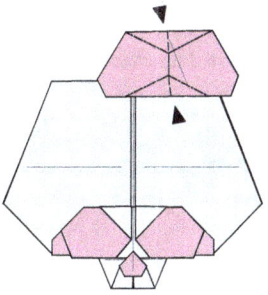

23. Push the sides in to make a 3-D bow.

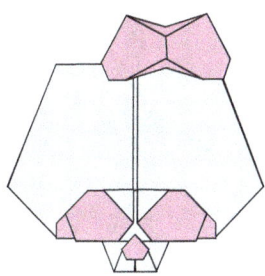

24. Completed *Skull with Bow*.

Ghost

People still claim to see physical incarnations of the dead, which are known as ghosts. A major social media company decided that using a logo of a spirit would be great to highlight how images on their site (allegedly) disappear. This emblem works well as an origami model with its simple form. Likewise, this paper *Ghost* is one of the easier pieces to fold in this collection.

ghost

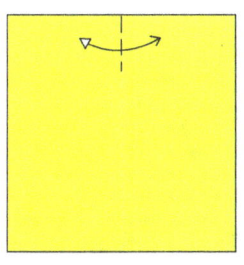 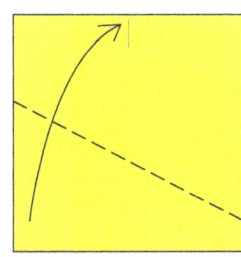 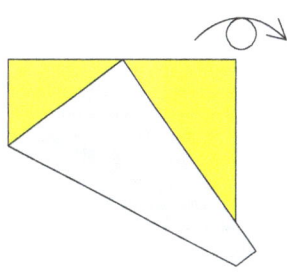

1. Precrease the edge in half.
2. Valley fold the corner to the crease.
3. Turn over.

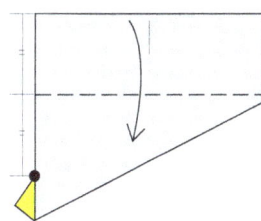 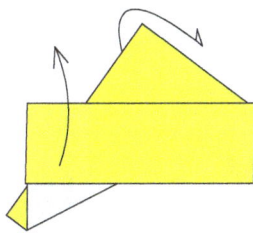 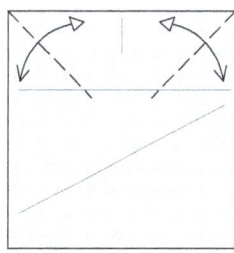

4. Valley fold to the dotted intersection.
5. Open out the pleat.
6. Precrease along the diagonals.

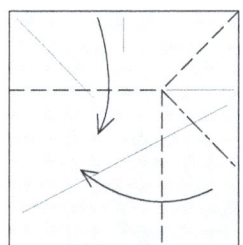 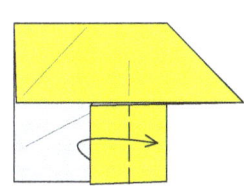 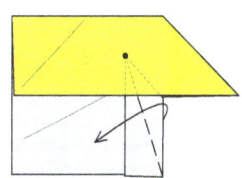

7. Rabbit ear the corner.
8. Lightly valley fold the top layer in half.
9. Valley fold starting from the hidden corner.

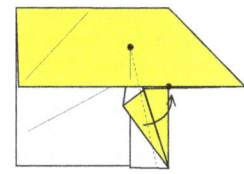 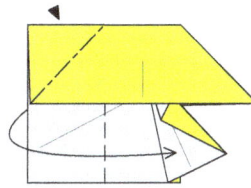 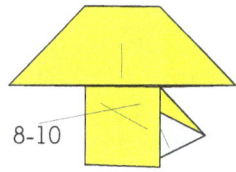

10. Slide the edge towards the dotted corner and flatten.
11. Reverse fold the edge over.
12. Repeat steps 8-10 in mirror image.

15

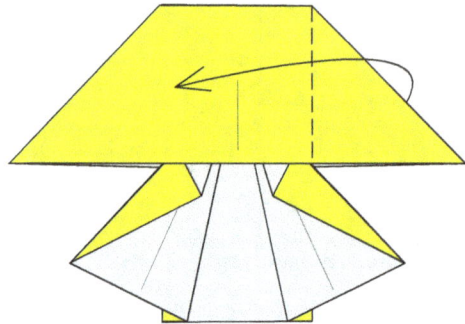

13. Valley fold the flap over.

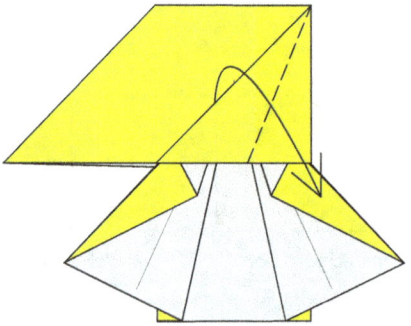

14. Valley fold down.

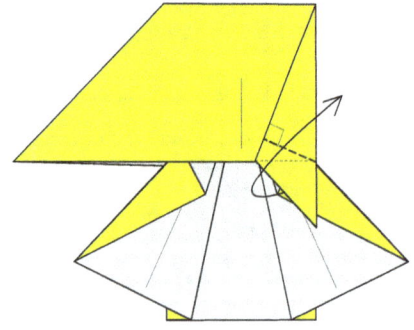

15. Valley fold the flap up, keeping the side edges aligned.

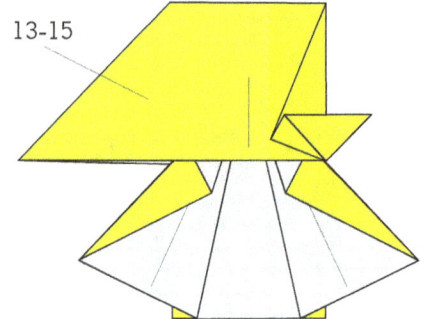

16. Repeat steps 13–15 in mirror image.

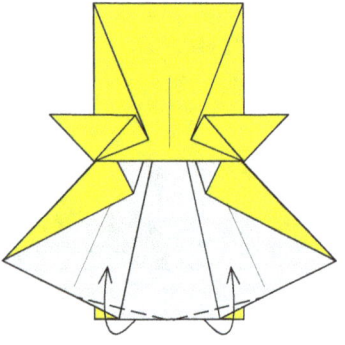

17. Valley fold the bottom edges up.

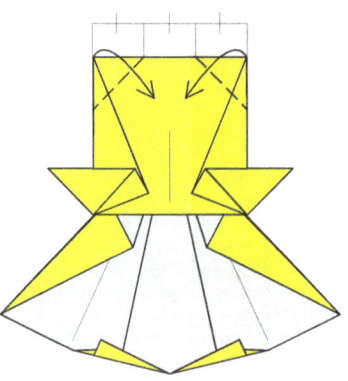

18. Valley fold the top corners in.

ghost

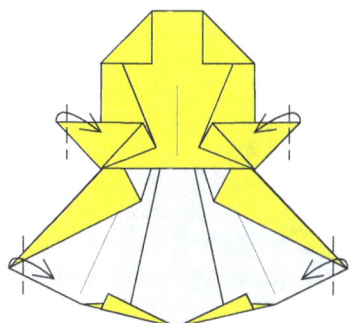

19. Valley fold the tips inwards.

20. Turn over.

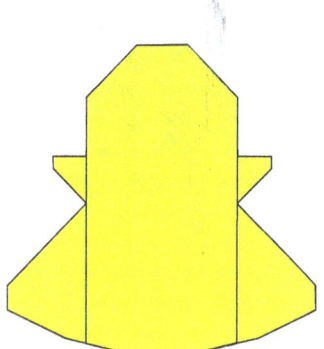

21. Completed *Ghost*.

Black Cat

Depending on which side of the globe you are on, black cats be considered lucky or the incarnation of pure evil. In North America, many believe it is bad luck to have one cross your path. Regardless of your feelings on the matter, seeing a black cat perched with an arched back and piercing eyes can be an intimidating sight. This is the pose used for this paper *Black Cat* and uses the classic Bird Base as its starting point.

black cat

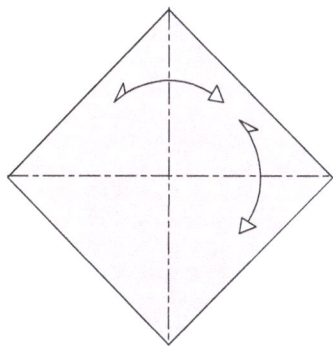

1. Precrease the diagonals with mountain folds.

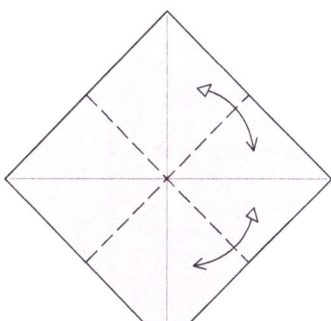

2. Precrease the sides in half.

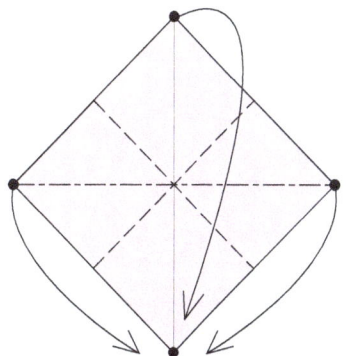

3. Bring the three corners to the bottom corner and collapse flat.

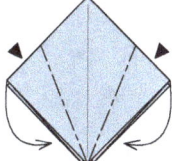

4. Reverse fold the sides.

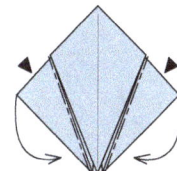

5. Reverse fold the rear flaps.

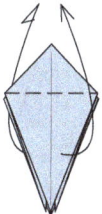

6. Swing the front and back flaps up.

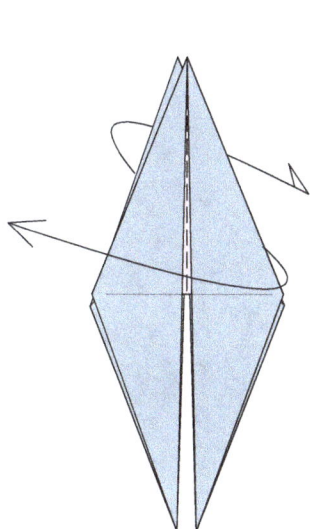

7. Swing over a flap at each side.

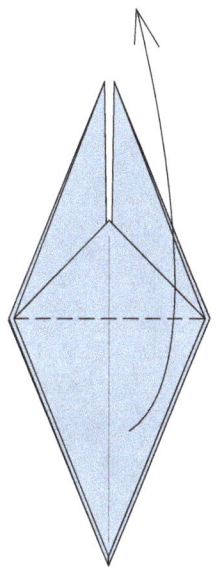

8. Lightly valley fold up.

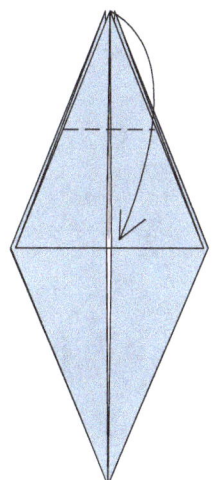

9. Valley fold to the center.

black cat

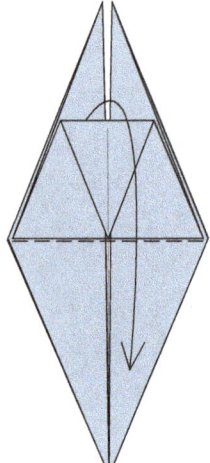 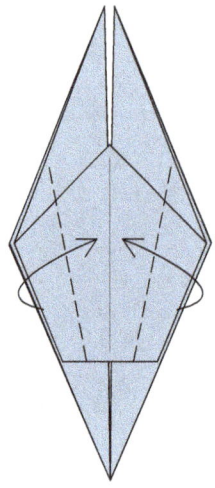 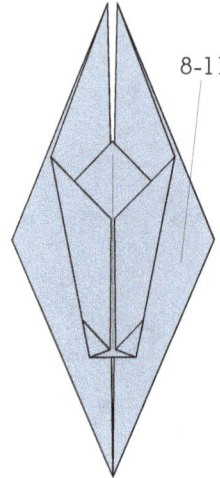

10. Swing the flap back down.
11. Valley fold the sides to the center.
12. Repeat steps 8-11 behind.

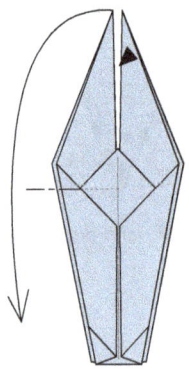 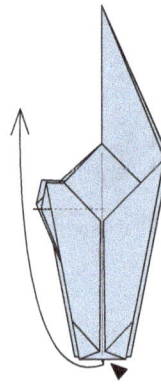 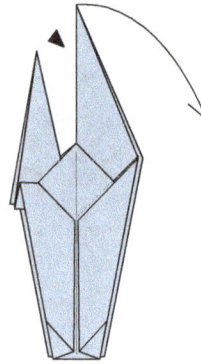

13. Reverse fold the flap straight down as far as possible.
14. Reverse fold the flap back up.
15. Reverse fold the flap outwards.

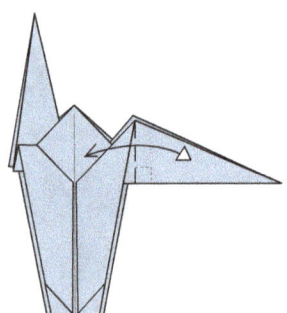 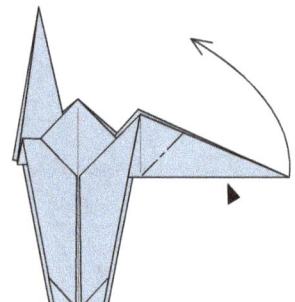 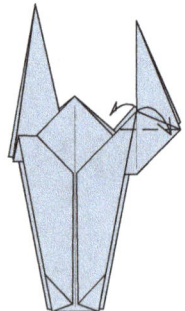

16. Precrease the flap.
17. Reverse fold the flap up.
18. Valley fold the corners down at each side.

black cat

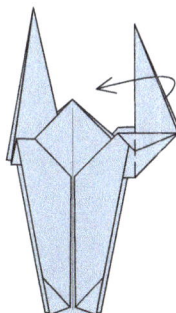

19. Open out the flap.

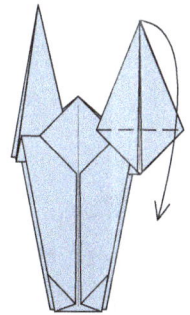

20. Valley fold down.

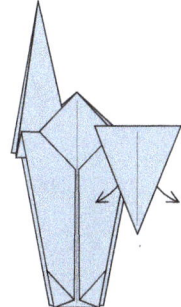

21. Slide out the side layers so the sides are straight.

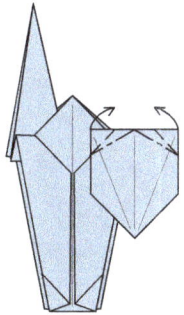

22. Pleat the corners at each side.

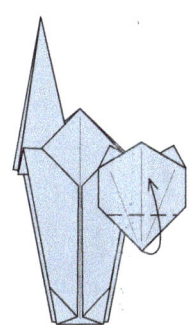

23. Valley fold the corner up.

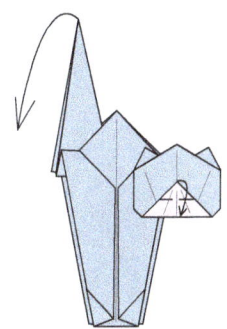

24. Valley fold down and curl the flap.

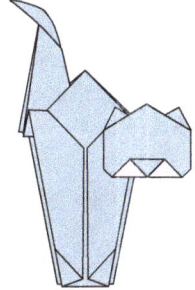

25. Completed *Black Cat*.

Bat

As coincidence would have it, bats happen to swarm for their last big meal in late October, making them a de facto icon of Halloween. Graphic artist Ellen Cohen depicted a vampire with exaggerated teeth, which this origami *Bat* is based on. Despite their proximity, these fangs are derived from opposite corners of the square.

bat

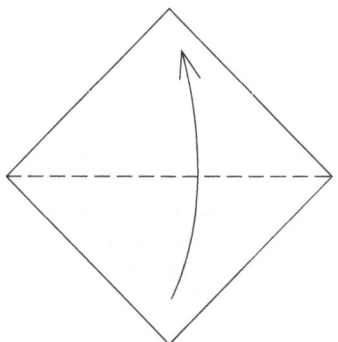

1. Valley fold in half along the diagonal.

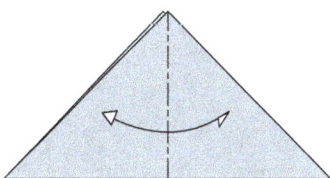

2. Precrease in half with a mountain fold.

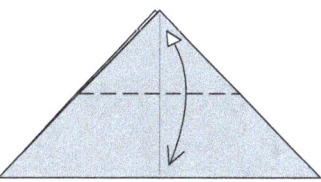

3. Precrease through both layers.

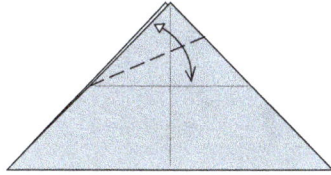

4. Precrease the top layer along the angle bisector.

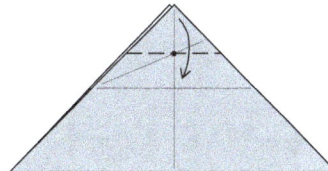

5. Valley fold through the dotted intersection.

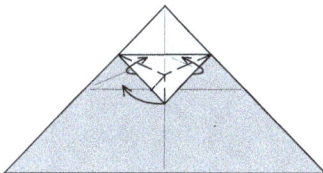

6. Rabbit ear the flap.

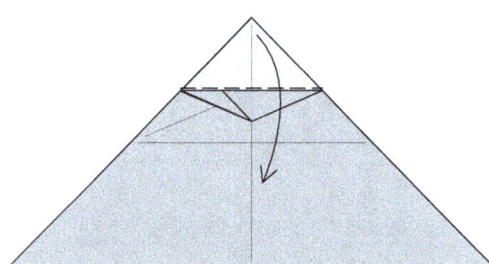

7. Valley fold the rear corner over.

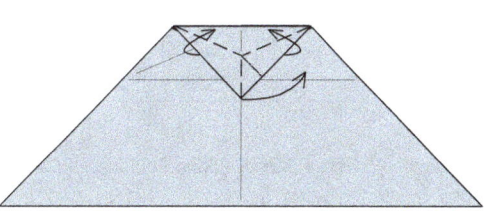

8. Rabbit ear the flap.

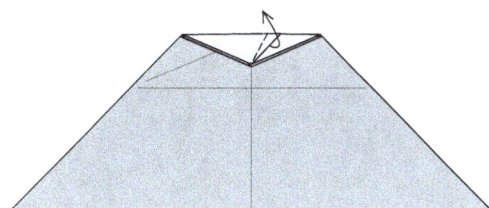

9. Valley fold the flap up, leaving a gap from the center of the model.

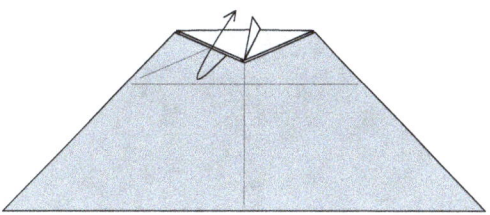

10. Pull the colored section around to the surface.

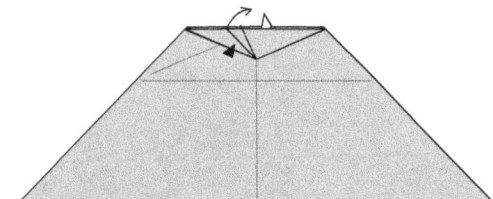

11. Reverse fold to match the angle of the other flap.

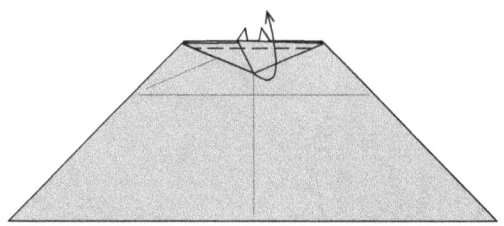

12. Valley fold the flap up so it covers the two small flaps.

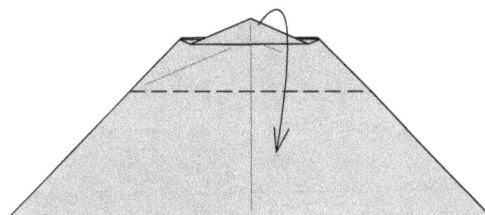

13. Valley fold along the existing crease.

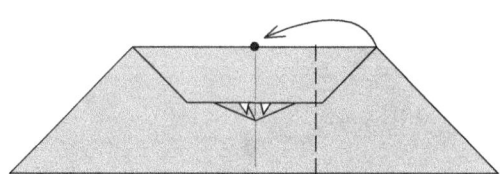

14. Valley fold so the corner hits the center crease.

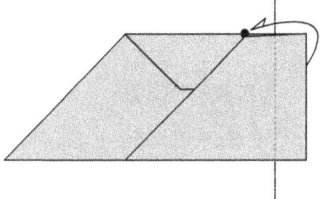

15. Mountain fold towards the dotted center, allowing the flap to flip outwards.

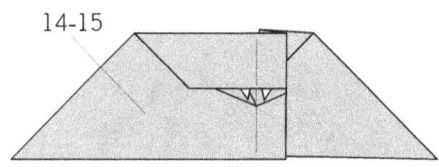

16. Repeat steps 14-15 in mirror image.

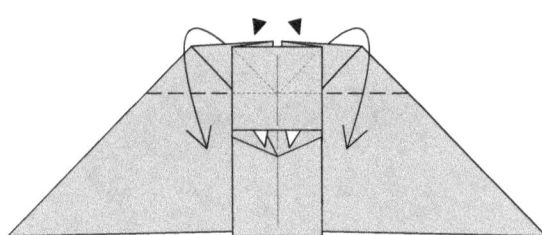

17. Swivel the edges down.

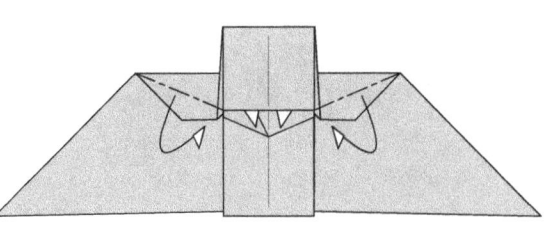

18. Mountain fold the edges inside.

bat

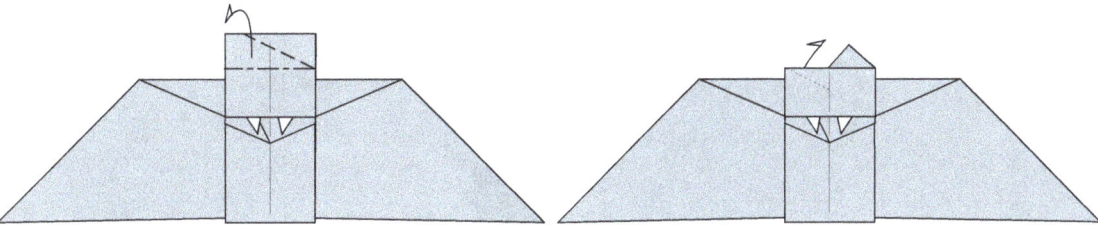

19. Pleat the top edge.

20. Pull up the opposite corner to match.

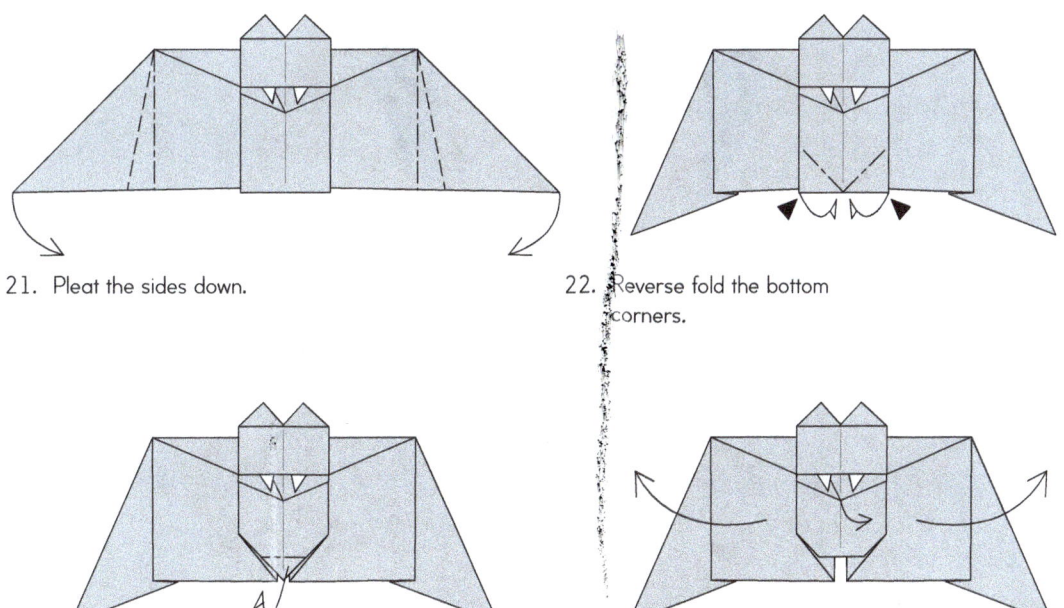

21. Pleat the sides down.

22. Reverse fold the bottom corners.

23. Mountain fold the corner.

24. Stretch apart the sides slightly and separate the head from the body.

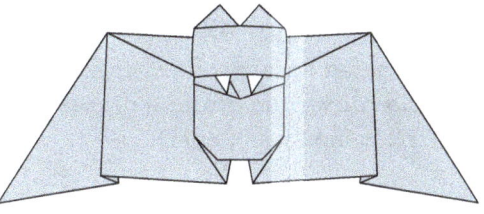

25. Completed *Bat*.

Jack-'o-lantern

Carving a face into a pumpkin serves the dual purpose of warding off evil spirits and doubling as a light source when a candle is placed inside. The Celtic people dubbed these creations *Jack-o'-lanterns* after the legend of a guy named Jack who was obligated to carry one after a sour deal with the devil. This origami version uses the darker side of the paper to depict the grimacing facial pattern.

jack-o'-lantern

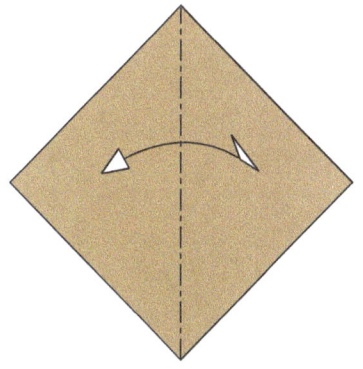

1. Precrease with a mountain fold.

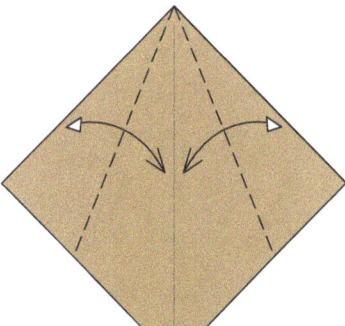

2. Precrease along the angle bisectors.

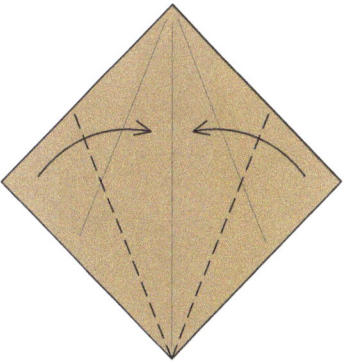

3. Valley fold the sides to the center.

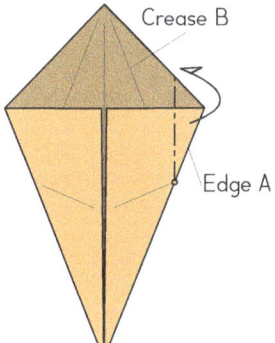

4. Mountain fold, such that edge A hits crease B.

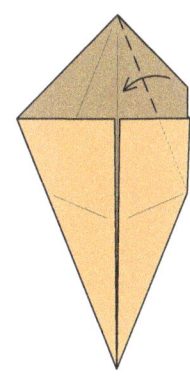

5. Valley fold along the existing crease.

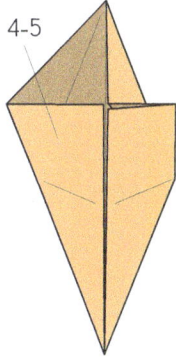

6. Repeat steps 4-5 in mirror image.

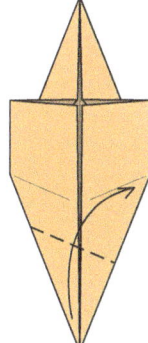

7. Valley fold to the corner.

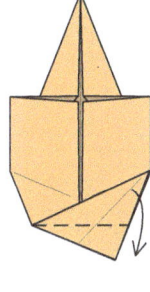

8. Valley fold down.

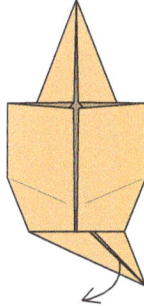

9. Unfold the pleat.

27

jack-o'-lantern

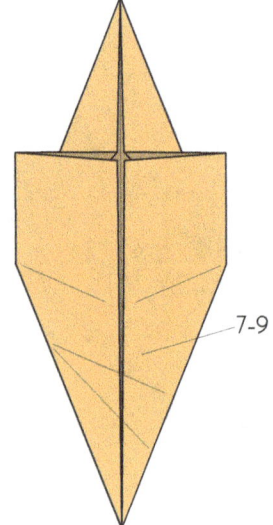
10. Repeat steps 7-9 in mirror image.

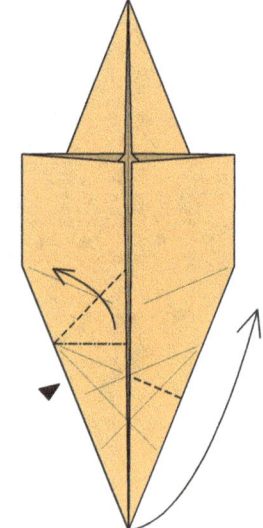
11. Squash fold.

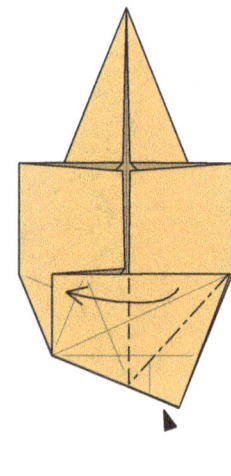
12. Squash fold.

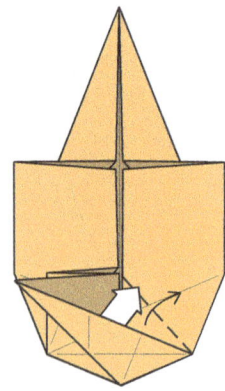
13. Pull out the single layer.

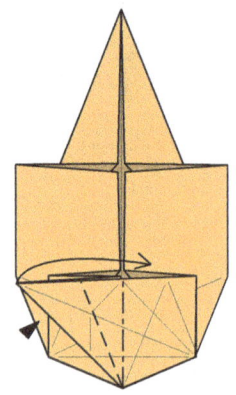
14. Crimp the center flap.

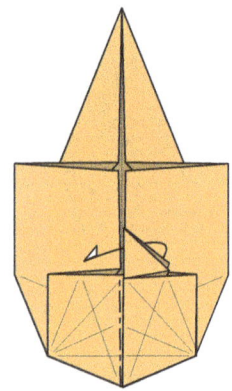
15. Swing the flap over.

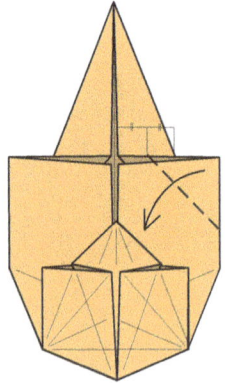
16. Valley fold.

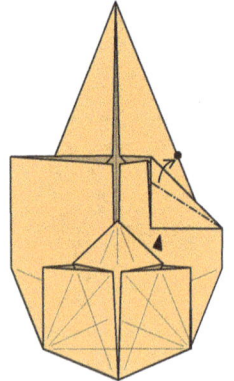
17. Squash fold.

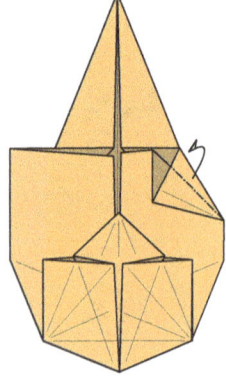
18. Mountain fold.

jack-o'-lantern

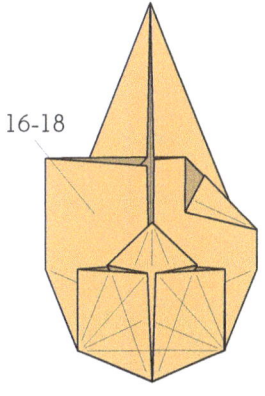

19. Repeat steps 16-18 in mirror image.

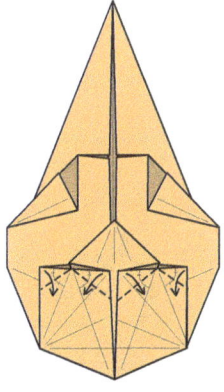

20. Valley fold the four flaps along the indicated angle bisectors.

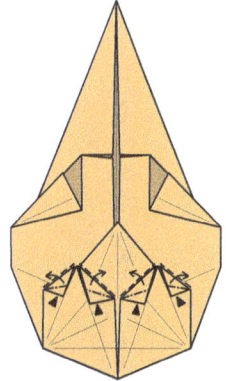

21. Squash fold the flaps.

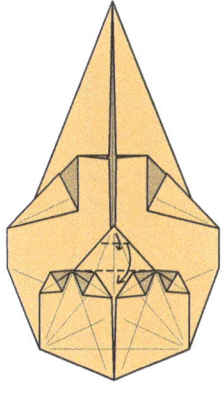

22. Valley fold the flap into the pocket.

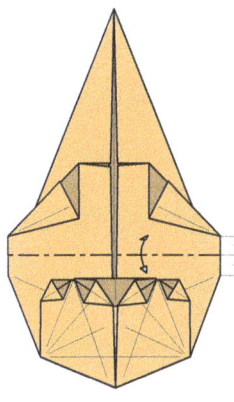

23. Precrease with a mountain fold.

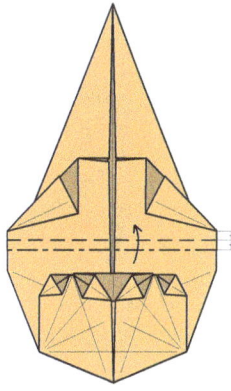

24. Pleat upwards.

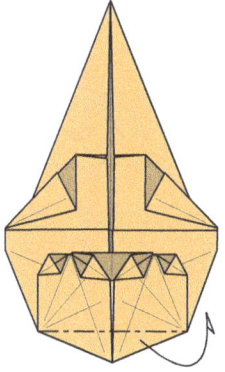

25. Mountain fold.

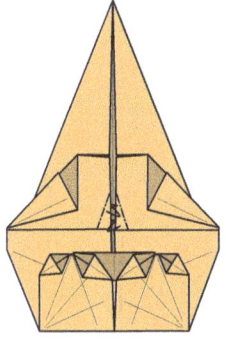

26. Swivel a single layer behind at each side.

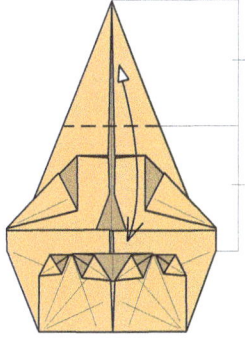

27. Precrease the top flap.

29

jack-o'-lantern

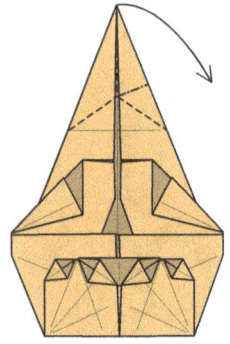

28. Rabbit ear.

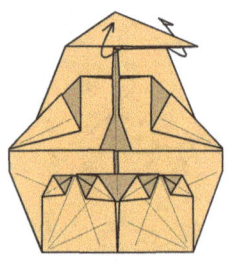

29. Wrap around a single layer at each side.

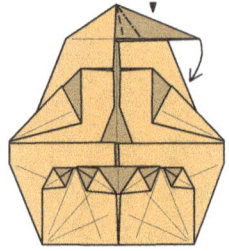

30. Squash fold asymmetrically.

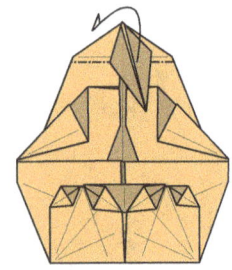

31. Mountain fold.

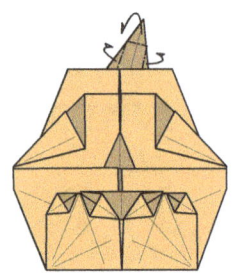

32. Mountain fold the edges.

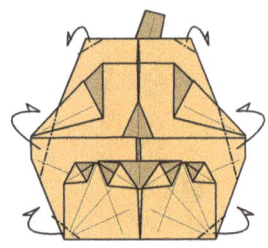

33. Mountain fold the corners.

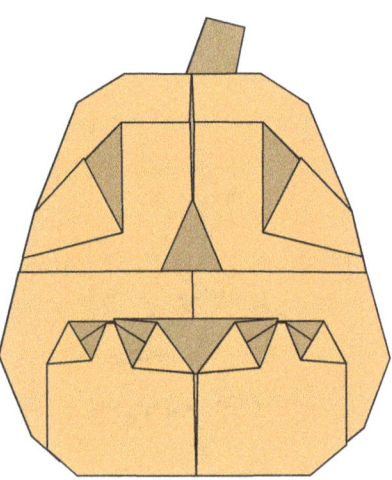

34. Completed *Jack-o'-lantern*.

Spider

Arachnophobia starts mysteriously in young children, perhaps because of a spider's many long legs moving haphazardly. Forming long limbs was the primary objective for this paper *Spider*. These appendages are conjoined at their root and fan out towards their ends with a subtle curl, giving an illusion of greater length.

spider

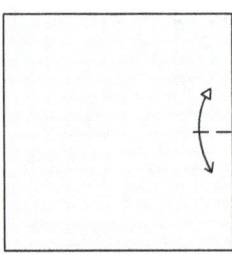

1. Precrease the edge in half.

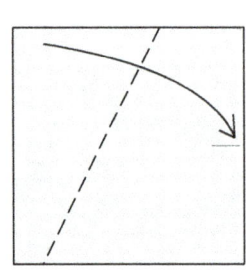

2. Valley fold the corner to the pinch mark.

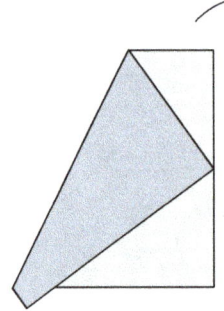

3. Turn over.

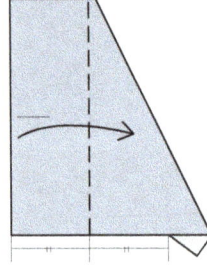

4. Valley fold so the bottom corner hits the intersection.

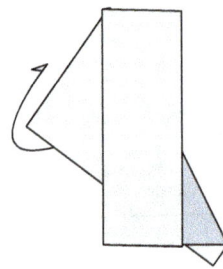

5. Unfold the rear section.

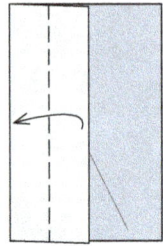

6. Valley fold the top section in half.

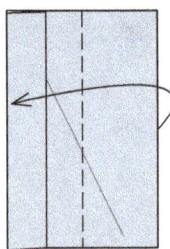

7. Valley fold over to the left.

8. Valley fold the top layer in half.

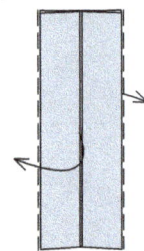

9. Open out the sides.

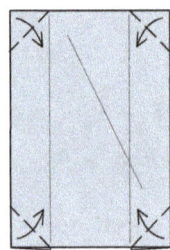

10. Valley fold the corners inwards.

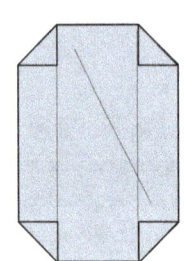

11. Turn over.

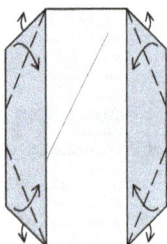

12. Valley fold the edges inwards, allowing the flaps from behind to swing forward.

spider

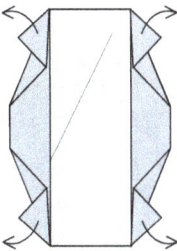
13. Unfold the four pleats.

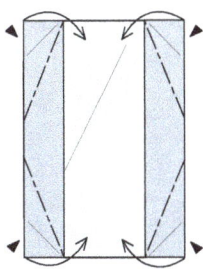
14. Reverse fold the corners in along the existing creases.

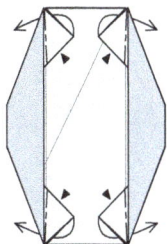
15. Reverse fold the four corners outwards.

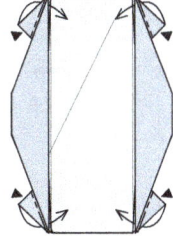
16. Reverse fold the corners in.

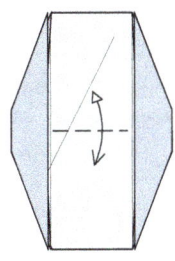
17. Precrease the middle section in half.

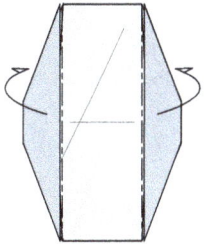
18. Mountain fold the sides behind.

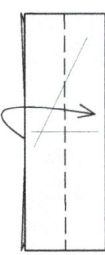
19. Valley fold in half.

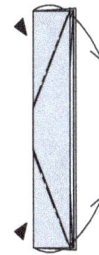
20. Reverse fold the center edges.

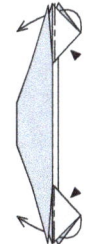
21. Reverse fold the corners outwards.

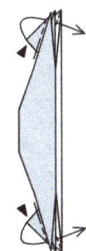
22. Reverse fold the corners inwards.

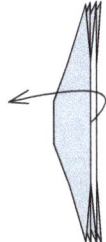
23. Open out the pleats along the center, returning to the position in step 19.

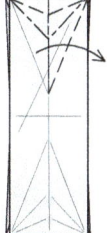
24. Replace the reverse folds at the top, swinging the resulting flap over. The model will be slightly concave.

spider

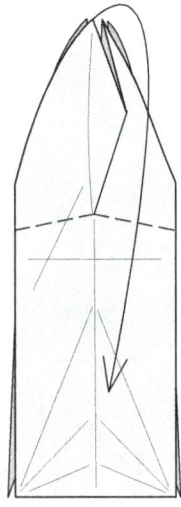

25. Squash the flap down to flatten.

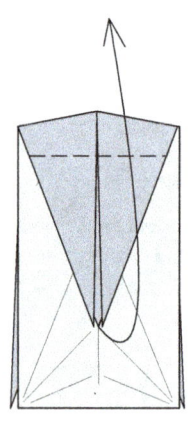

26. Valley fold up, to align with the center crease underneath.

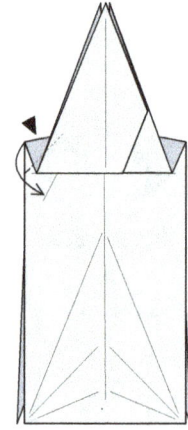

27. Reverse fold the corner.

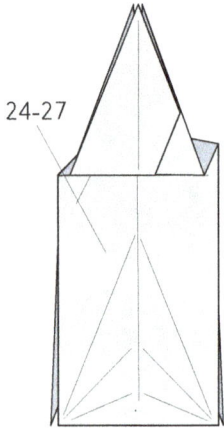

28. Repeat steps 24-27 at the bottom.

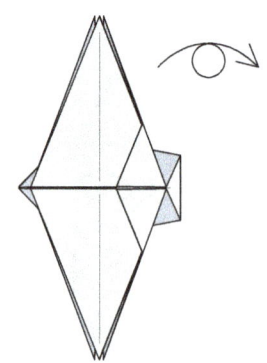

29. Turn over.

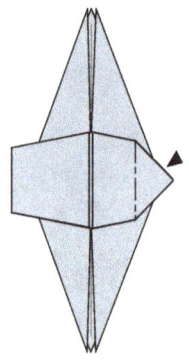

30. Reverse fold the flap.

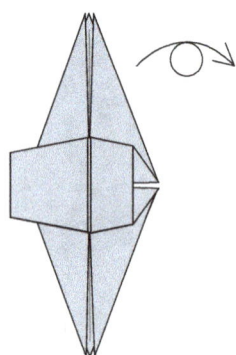

31. Turn over.

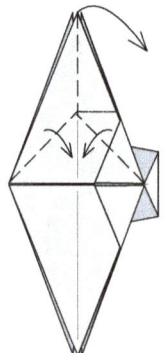

32. Rabbit ear the flap.

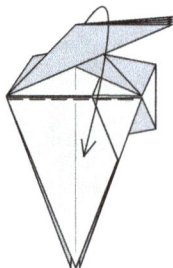

33. Swing the flap down.

spider

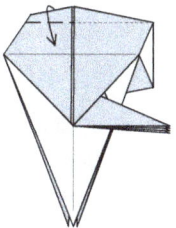

34. Valley fold the edge down. Part of the fold is hidden.

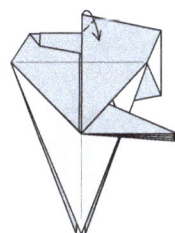

35. Valley fold the corner.

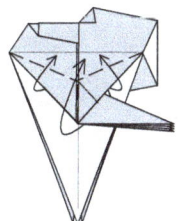

36. Rabbit ear the flap up.

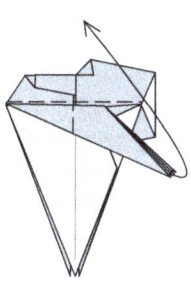

37. Swing the cluster of flaps over, so that it stands straight up.

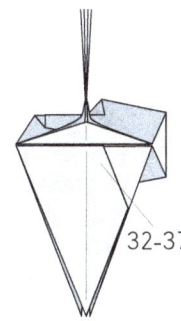

38. Repeat steps 32-37 at the bottom.

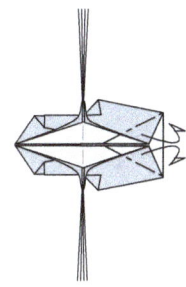

39. Mountain fold the corners inside to lock.

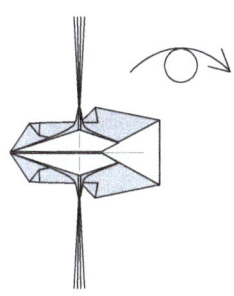

40. Turn over.

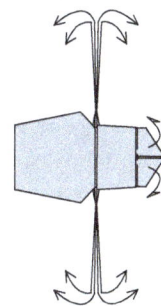

41. Fold the flaps down slightly and curl the legs outwards.

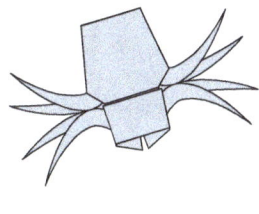

42. Completed *Spider*.

Alien

Just before the space race of the 1960's, people's imaginations went wild with what sorts of intelligent life might lie in outer space, along with equally outrageous fears on how they might take over our poor planet. It is logical to assume that life exists beyond Earth given the incredible vastness of the universe. While the shape and form of such extraterrestrial creatures are yet to be determined, most depictions have a strong kinship to our own human form.

This origami incarnation has borrowed a few features from some famous aliens, with proportions that appeal to our love of infants with large heads and wide eyes.

alien

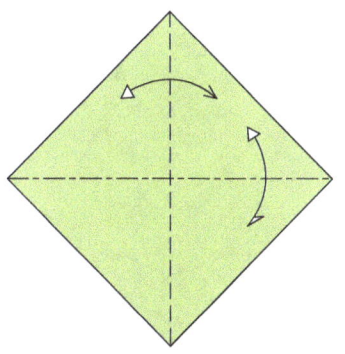

1. Precrease in half along the diagonals with mountain and valley folds.

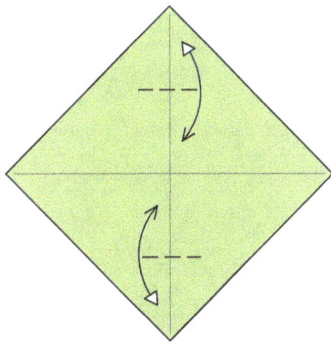

2. Make pinch marks at the midway points.

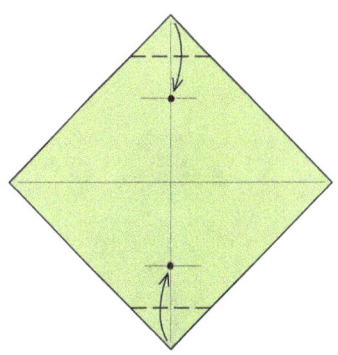

3. Valley fold the corners to the dotted intersections.

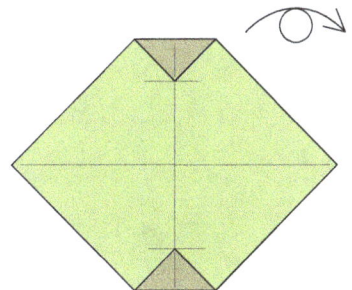

4. Turn over.

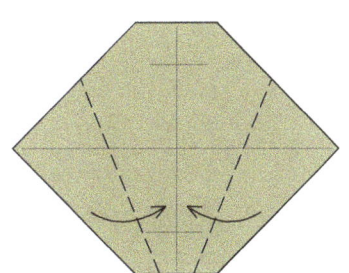

5. Valley fold the sides to the center.

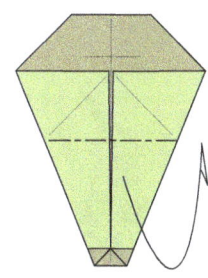

6. Mountain fold in half.

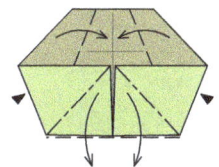

7. Valley fold the sides to the center, allowing the corners to squash down.

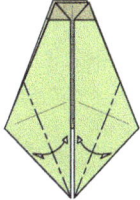

8. Precrease with mountain folds.

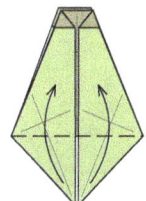

9. Valley fold the flaps up.

37

alien

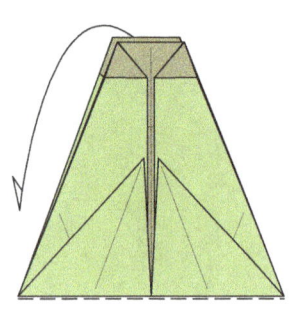

10. Swing the rear flap down.

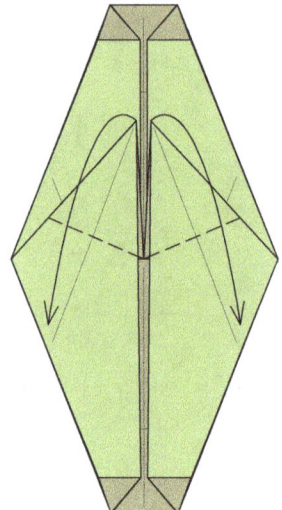

11. Valley fold the flaps outwards so that their outer edges lie straight.

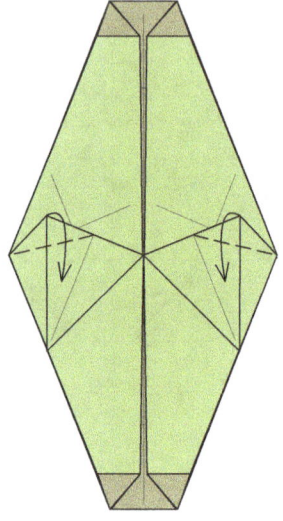

12. Valley fold the corners, aligning with the creases.

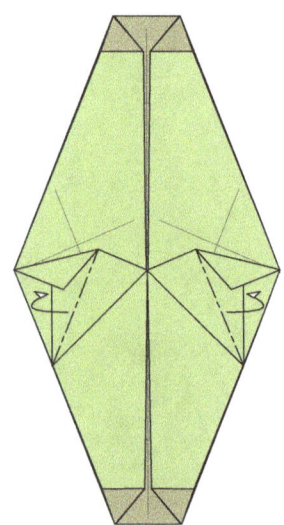

13. Mountain fold along the existing creases and press flat.

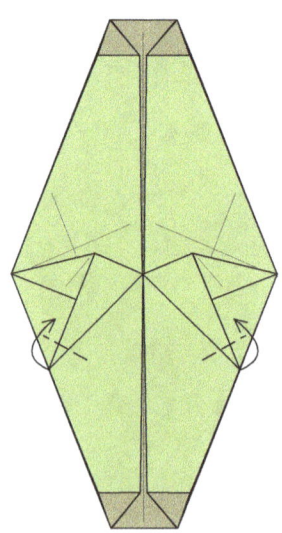

14. Outside reverse fold the corners, distributing the layers to reveal the inner color.

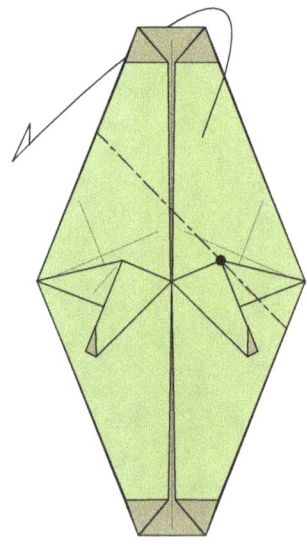

15. Mountain fold, ensuring the fold passes through the dotted point.

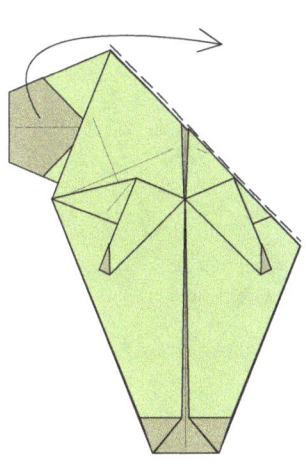

16. Note that the flap lies horizontal. Unfold the flap.

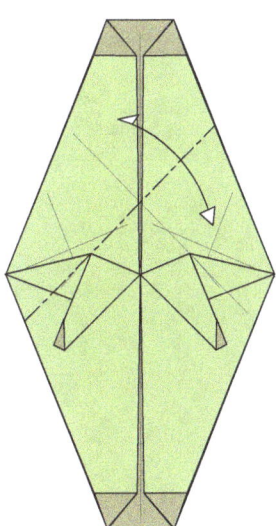

17. Repeat the precrease from steps 15-16 in the opposite direction.

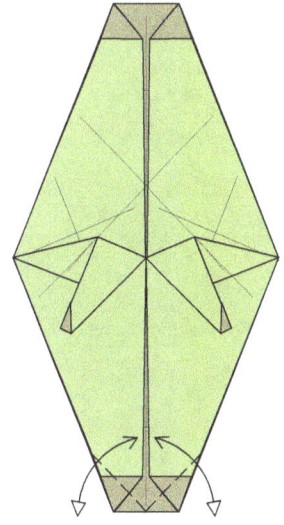

18. Precrease along the angle bisectors.

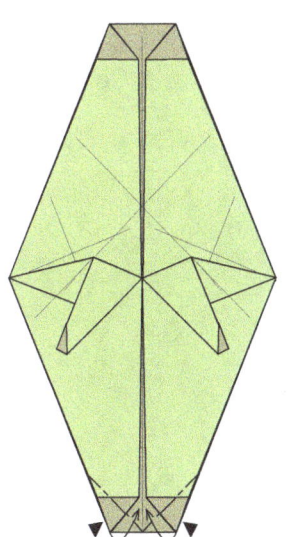

19. Reverse fold the corners.

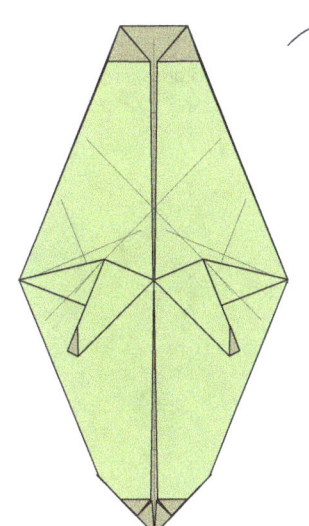

20. Turn over.

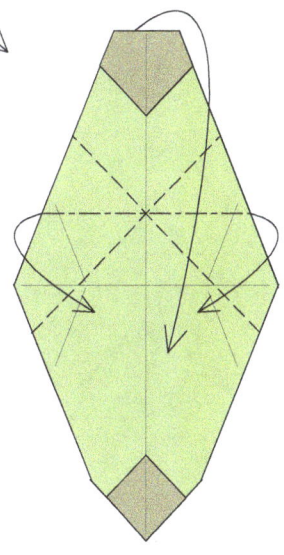

21. Bring the flap down while reverse folding the sides.

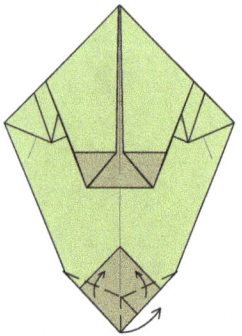

22. Rabbit ear the corner.

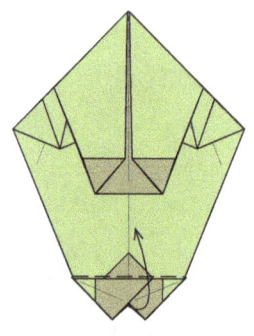

23. Valley fold the bottom section up.

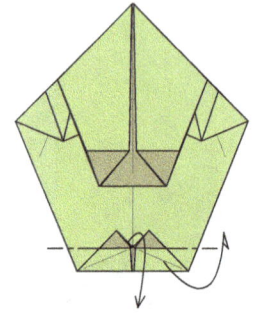

24. Mountain fold, allowing the top section to flip down.

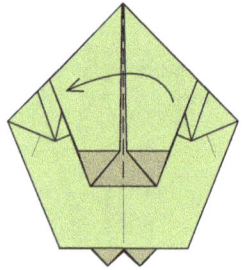

25. Swing over one flap.

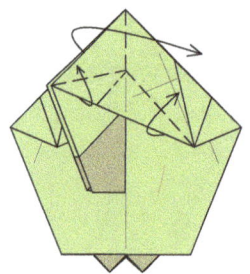

26. Swing the flap back while incorporating a reverse fold.

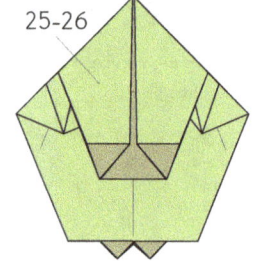

27. Repeat steps 25-26 in mirror image.

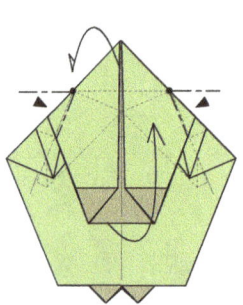

28. Flip the flap starting from the hidden dotted points. Allow the corners of the flap to squash flat.

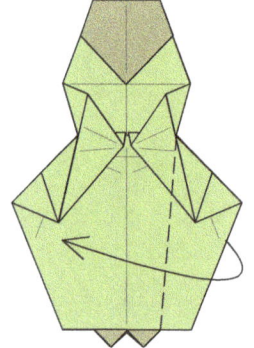

29. Valley fold over.

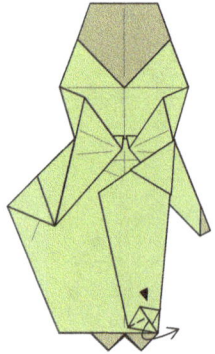

30. Squash the pleated section outwards.

a l i e n

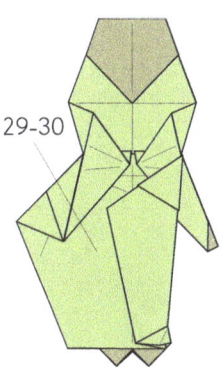 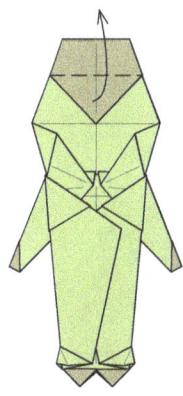 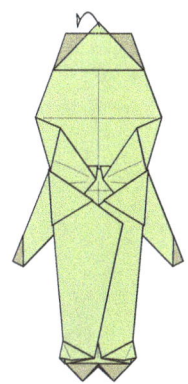

31. Repeat steps 29-30 in mirror image.

32. Valley fold the corner up.

33. Mountain fold the tip behind.

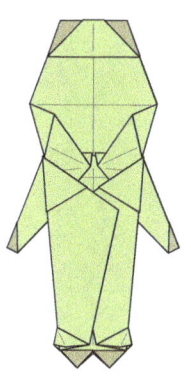 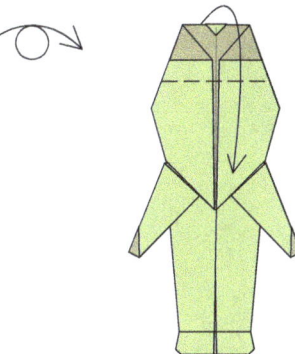 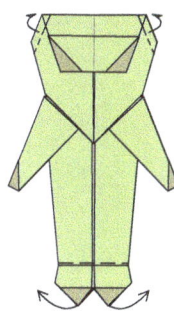

34. Turn over.

35. Valley fold down.

36. Mountain fold the edges. Raise the feet out strait so that the model will stand.

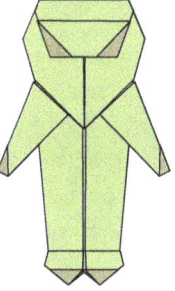

37. Completed *Alien*.

Witch

Witches are believed to be on the darker side of religion, practicing Devil worship and using their metaphysical powers to cast evil spells. The way they have been depicted throughout history has changed along with our fear and fascination with the occult. This paper *Witch* sports the quintessential broomstick and pointed hat that has been associated with the modern archetype.

witch

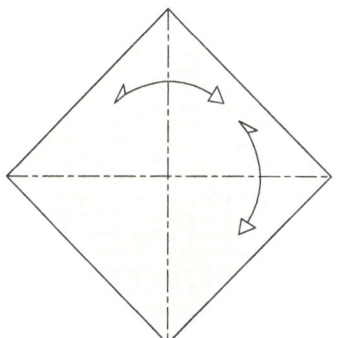

1. Precrease the diagonals with mountain folds.

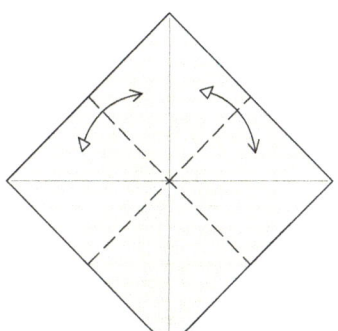

2. Precrease the sides in half.

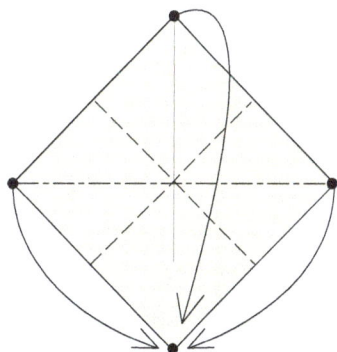

3. Collapse the corners down.

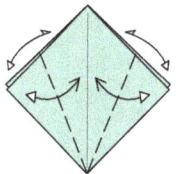

4. Precrease the sides along the angle bisectors.

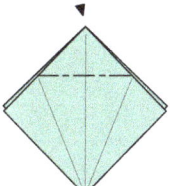

5. Sink the top corner.

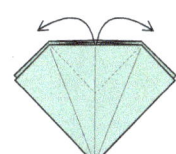

6. Reverse fold the hidden corners outwards.

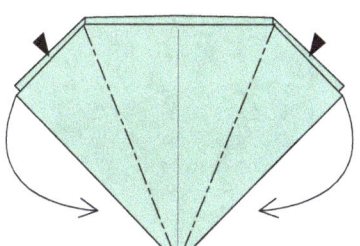

7. Reverse fold the sides.

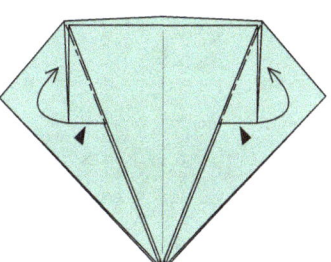

8. Reverse fold the corners.

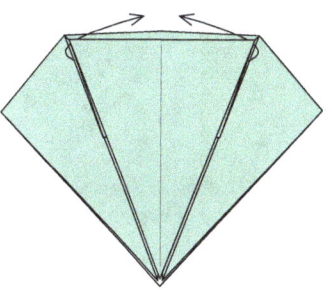

9. Undo the hidden reverse folds.

witch

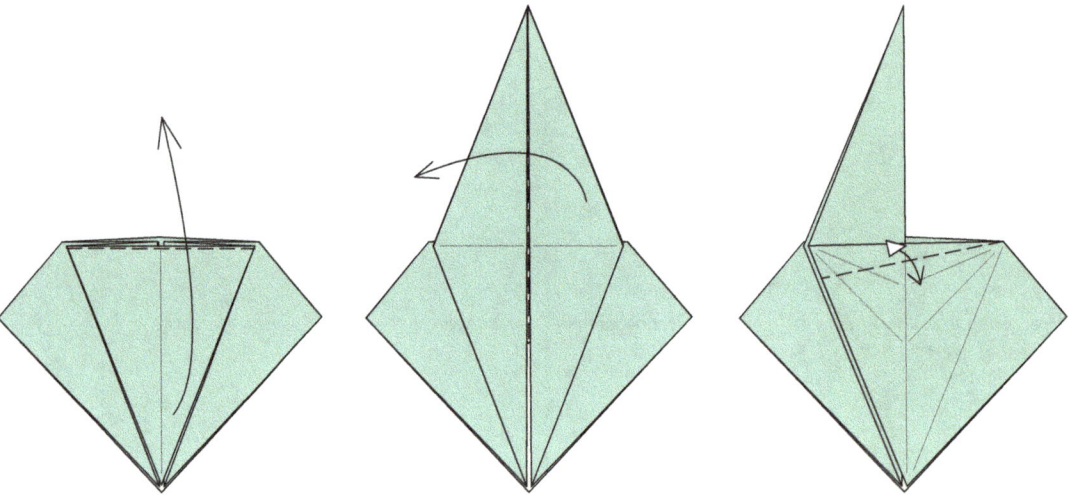

10. Swing the top flap up.

11. Swing over one flap.

12. Precrease along the angle bisector.

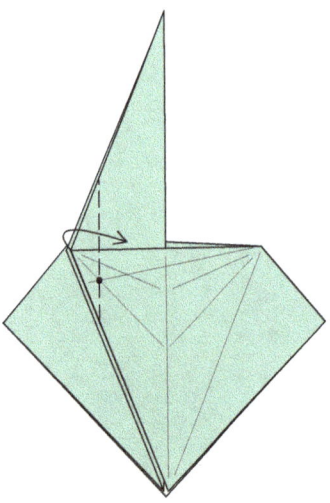

13. Valley fold through the dotted intersection of creases.

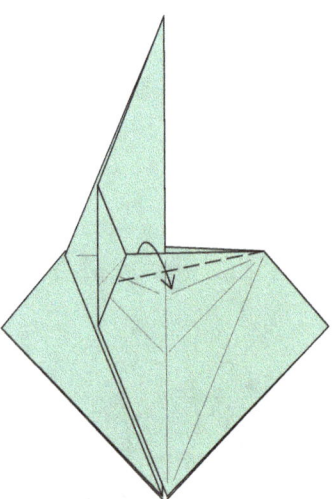

14. Valley fold, allowing a swivel to form.

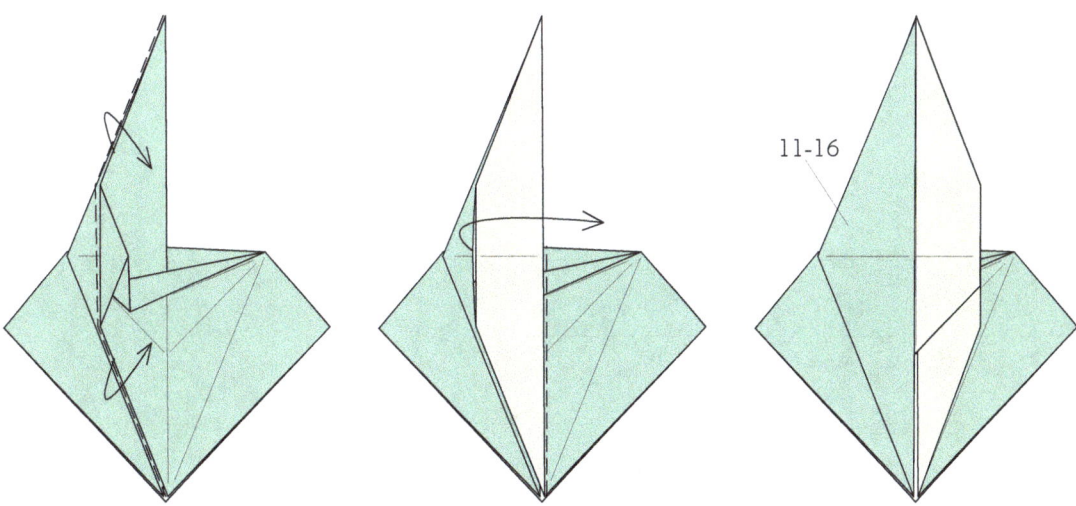

15. Wrap around a single layer.

16. Swing over one flap.

17. Repeat steps 11-16 in mirror image.

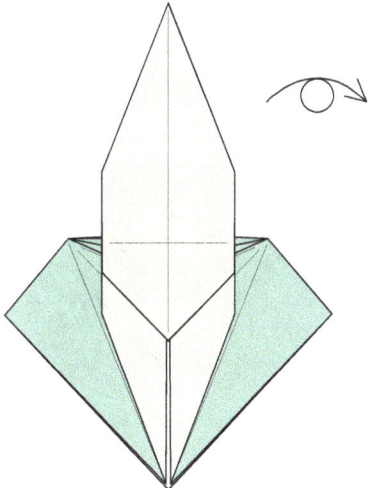

18. Turn over.

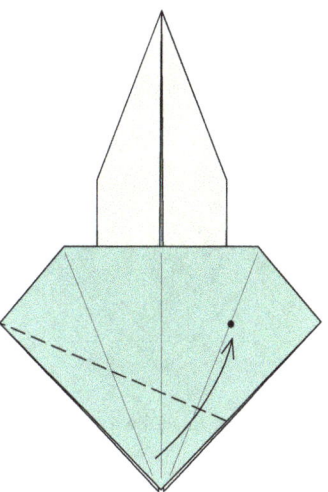

19. Valley fold the corner to the crease.

witch

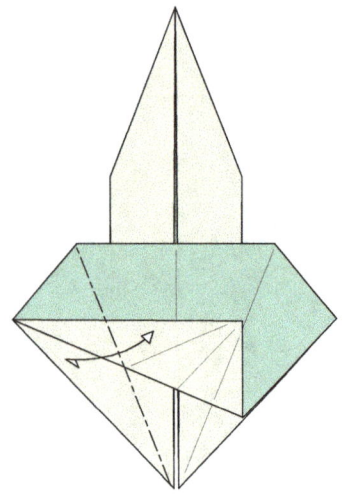

20. Precrease along the existing crease.

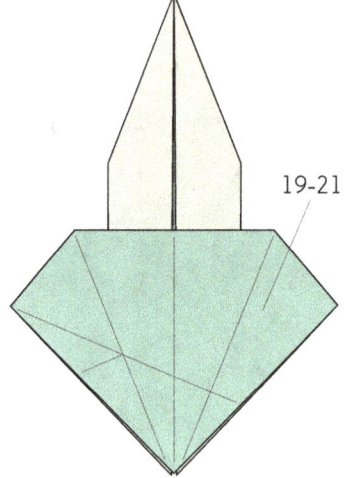

21. Unfold the flap.

22. Repeat steps 19-21 in mirror image.

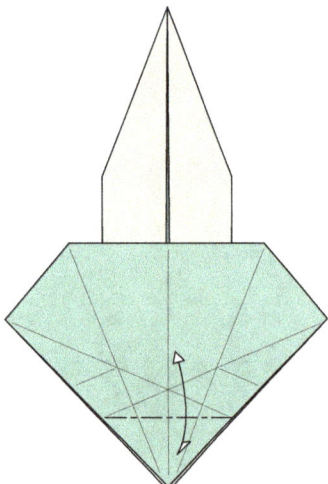

23. Precrease the top layer.

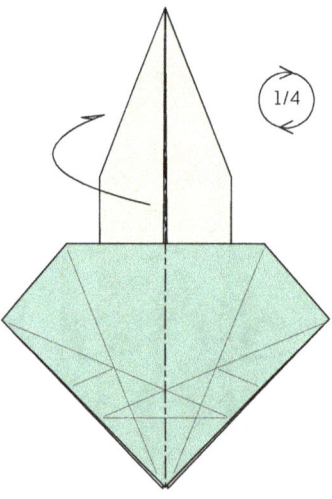

24. Mountain fold in half and rotate.

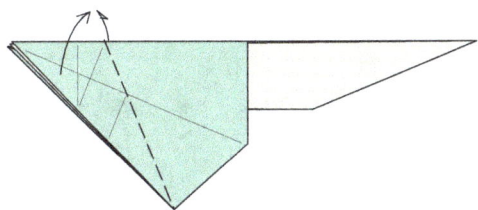

25. Outside reverse fold.

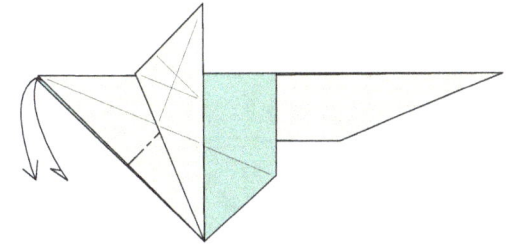

26. Lightly mountain fold the flaps out of the way.

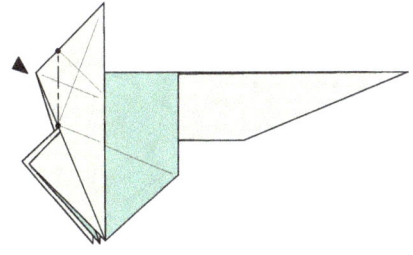

27. Sink the corner.

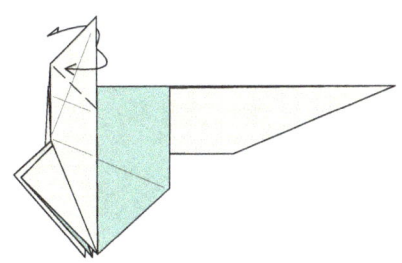

28. Outside reverse fold.

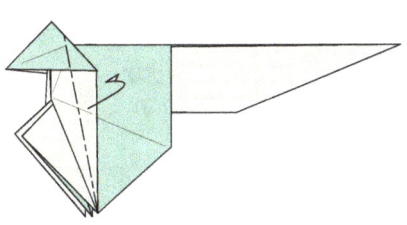

29. Mountain fold at each side along the angle bisector.

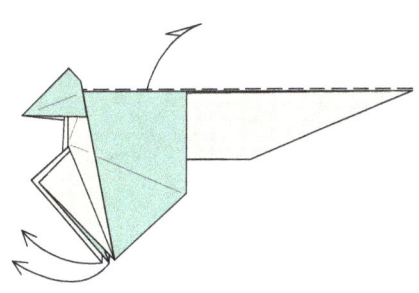

30. Open out along the center, unfolding the bottom flaps. The center flap will not flatten completely.

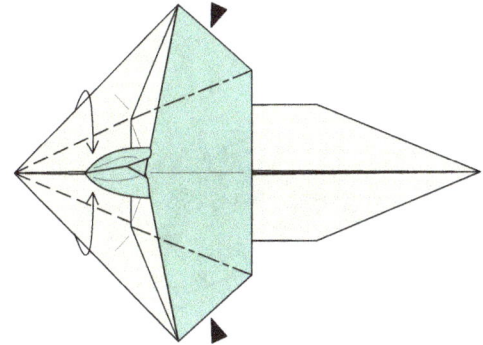

31. Reverse fold the sides.

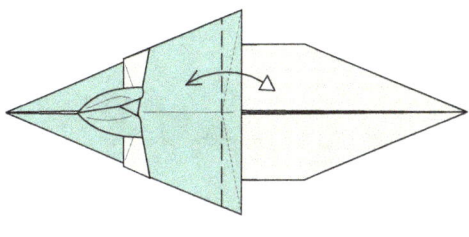

32. Precrease starting from the hidden joint.

witch

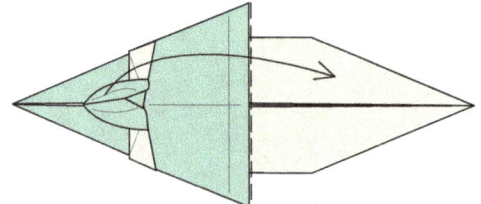

33. Open out the top flap.

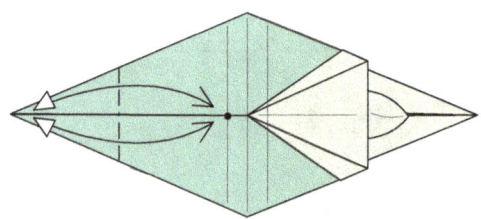

34. Precrease to the dotted intersection.

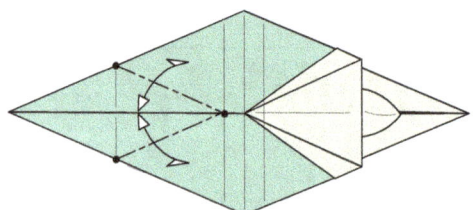

35. Precrease with mountain folds.

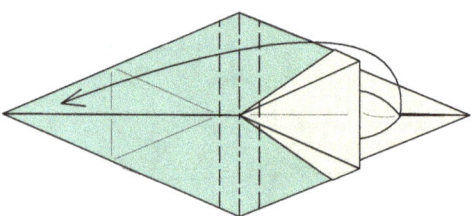

36. Swing the flap back over. inserting a pleat.

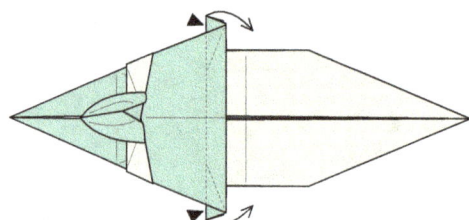

37. Reverse fold the corners over.

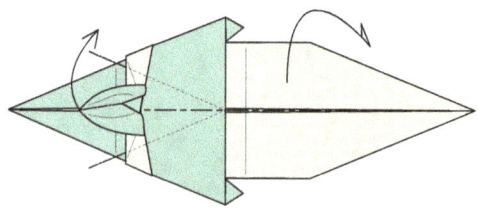

38. Mountain fold in half while crimping the left side up.

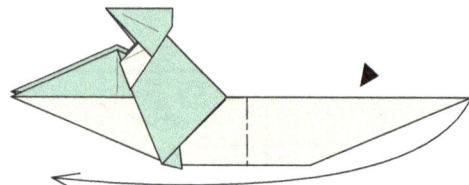

39. Reverse fold the flap.

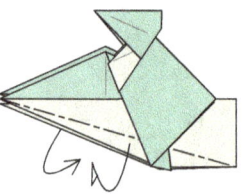

40. Mountain fold the outer edges inside.

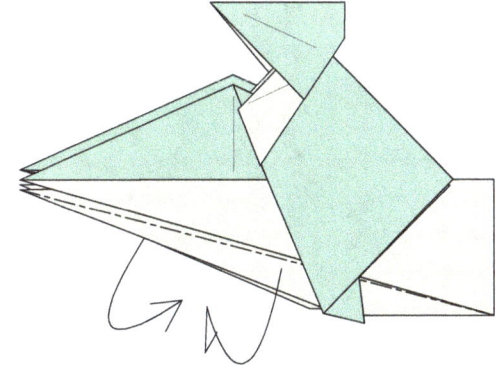

41. Mountain fold the edges inside.

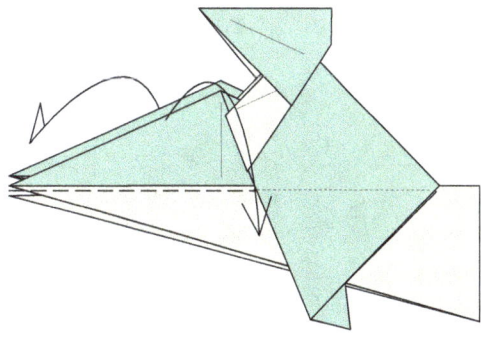

42. Valley fold the colored flaps down at each side.

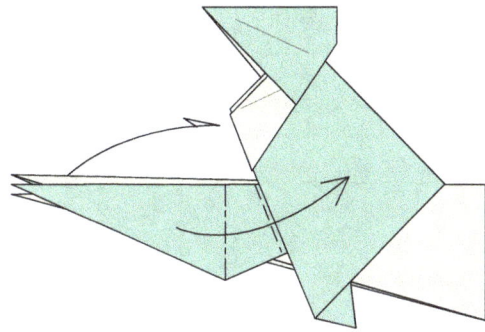

43. Pleat the side flaps up.

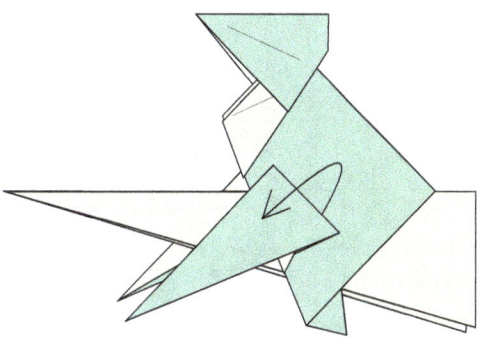

44. Tuck the flaps inside, locking their top corners under the hidden hems.

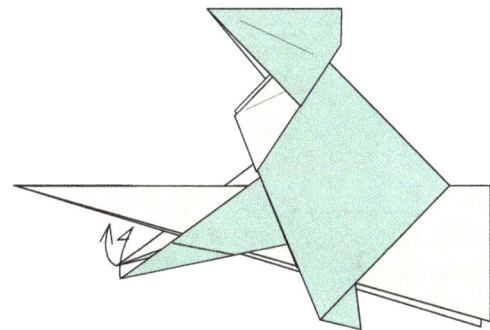

45. Tuck the corners inside, wrapping them around the hidden edges for a better lock.

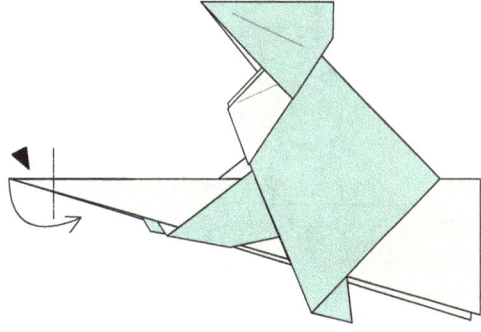

46. Reverse fold the tip.

witch

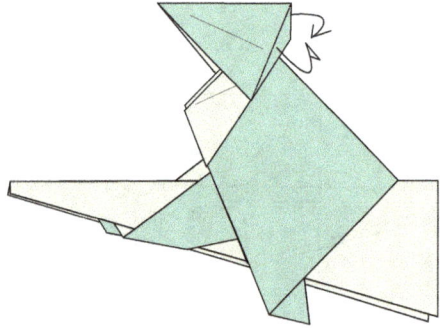

47. Mountain fold the side edges inside.

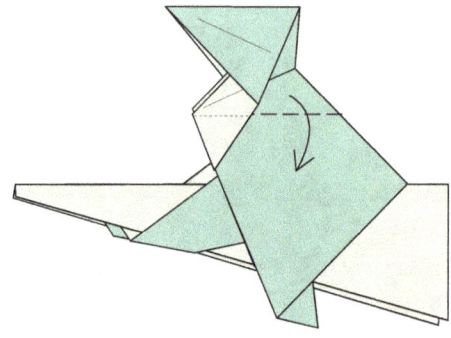

48. Valley fold down, releasing the trapped paper.

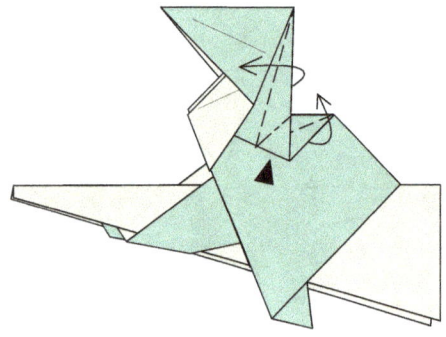

49. Swivel fold.

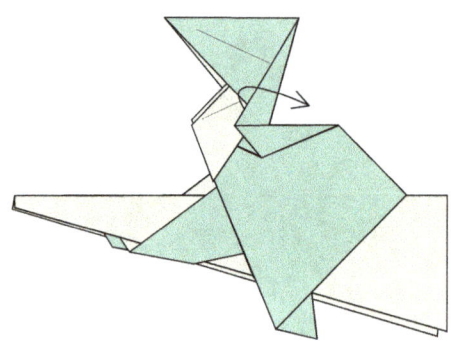

50. Wrap around a layer to the surface.

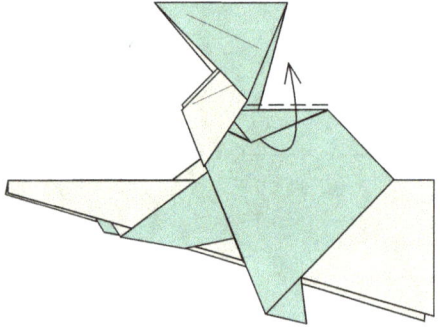

51. Swing the corner up.

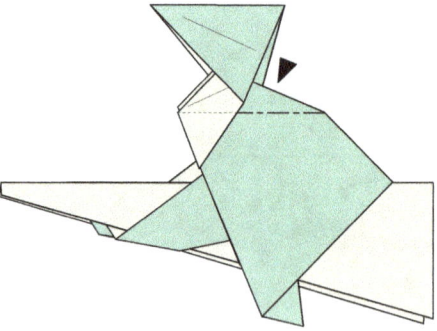

52. Closed sink the corner.

witch

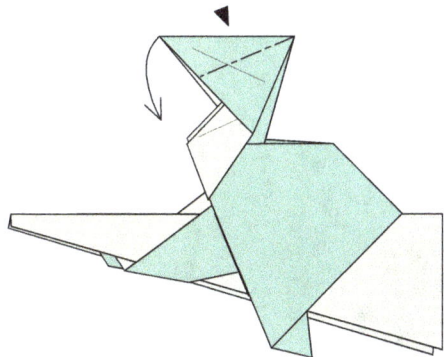

53. Reverse fold the corner.

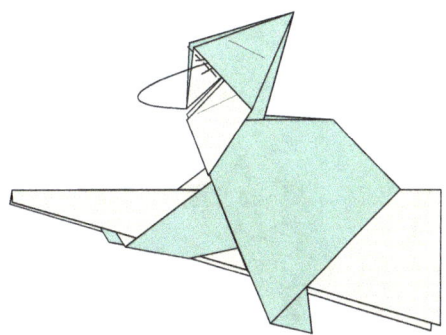

54. Tuck the corner inside.

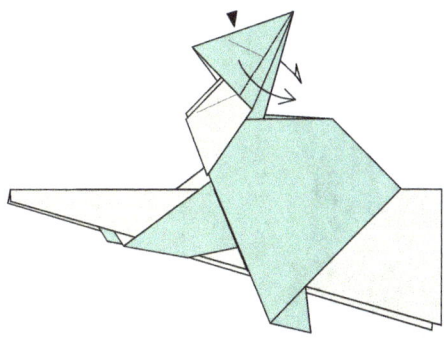

55. Slide the layers over and flatten.

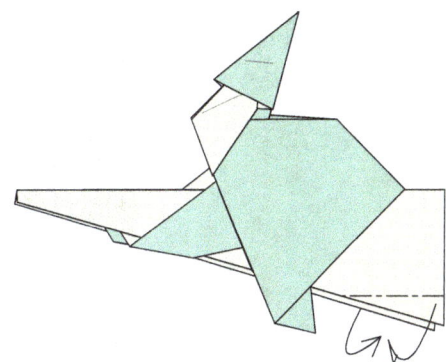

56. Mountain fold the bottom corners and interlock them to make the broom 3-D.

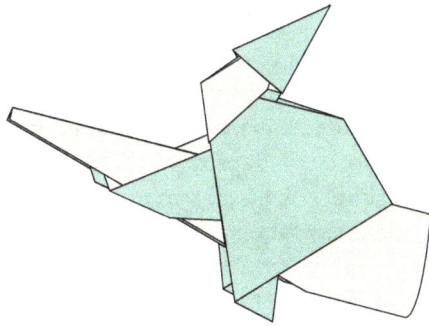

57. Completed *Witch*.

Grim Reaper

The concept of death has fascinated people throughout history, so it comes as no surprise that it would be personified like other mythological explanations to naturally occurring phenomena. In the West, the depiction would be a human figure with a gaunt (or simply skeletal) frame wearing a dark robe. He would wield a scythe, which sports a blade sharp enough to sever the soul from the body. This origami *Grim Reaper* follows this , using a set of flaps from the classic Frog Base to form his weapon.

grim reaper

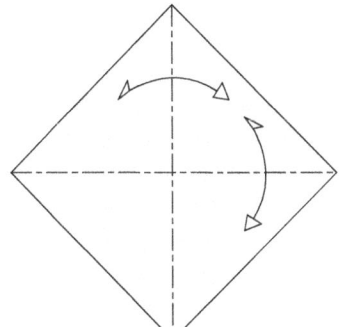

1. Precrease the diagonals with mountain folds.

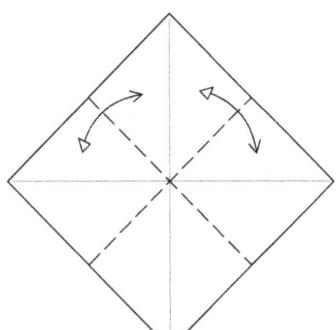

2. Precrease the sides in half.

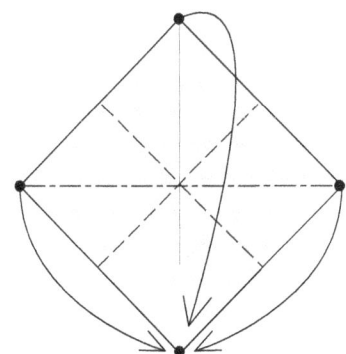

3. Collapse the corners down.

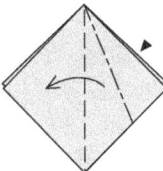

4. Squash the side corner.

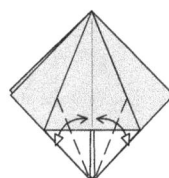

5. Precrease along the angle bisectors.

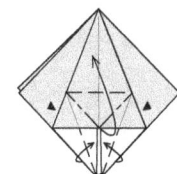

6. Petal fold up.

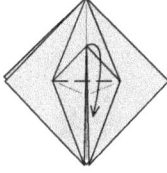

7. Valley fold the flap down.

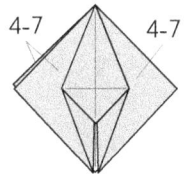

8. Repeat steps 4-7 on the remaining three flaps.

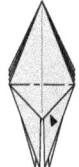

9. Reverse fold the corner inside.

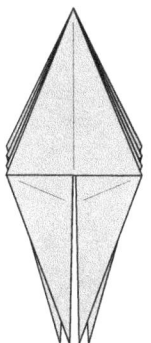

10. Turn over.

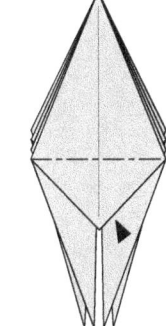

11. Reverse fold the corner inside.

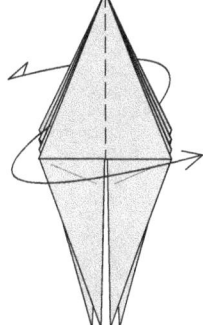

12. Swing over two flaps at each side.

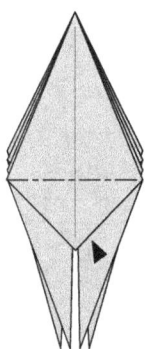
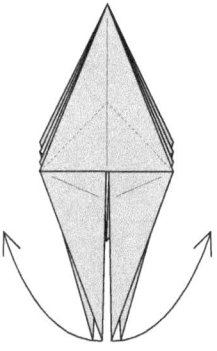
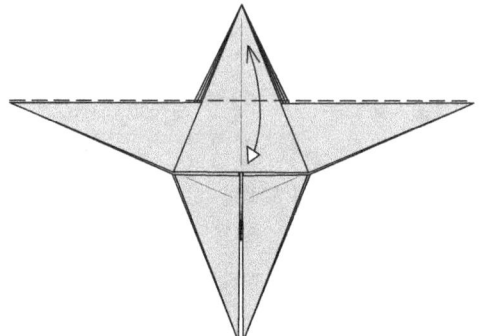

13. Reverse fold the corner inside.

14. Reverse fold the top flaps outwards.

15. Swing the top layer up and then down to create a precrease.

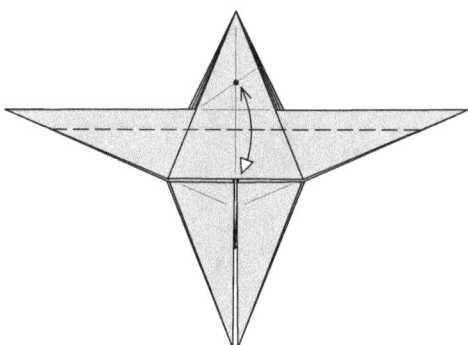

16. Precrease along the angle bisector.

17. Precrease the top layer towards the dotted intersection of creases.

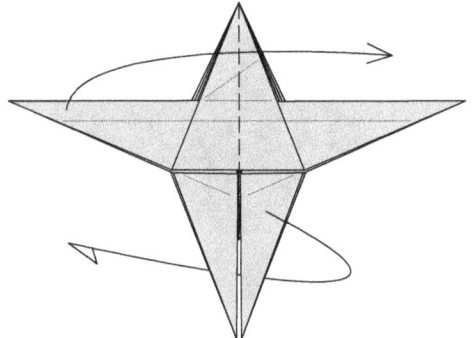
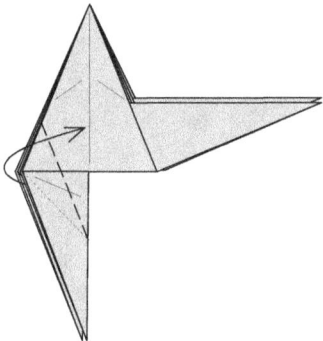

18. Swing over a flap at each side.

19. Valley fold the two flaps along the hidden angle bisector.

grim reaper

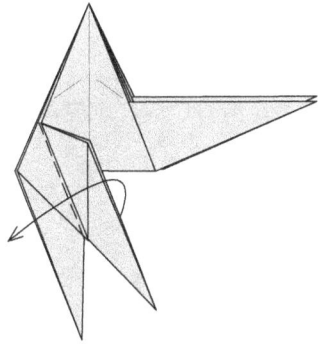

20. Swing back the two flaps.

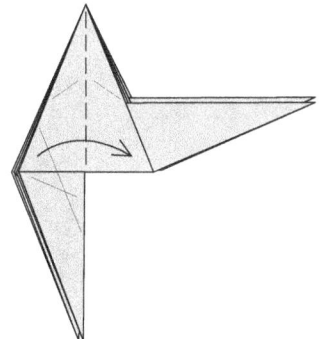

21. Swing over one flap.

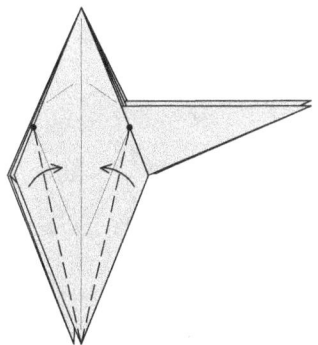

22. Valley fold the sides, starting from the dotted intersections.

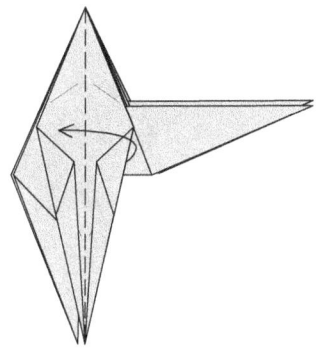

23. Swing the flap back over.

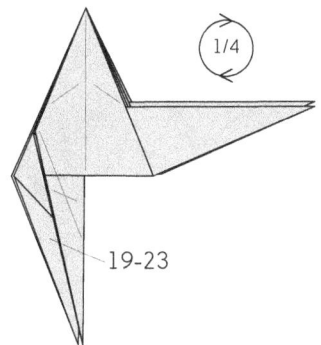

24. Repeat steps 19-23 behind. Rotate the model 1/4 turn.

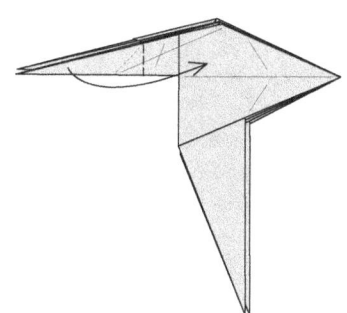

25. Valley fold over as far as possible, starting from the tip of the hidden flap.

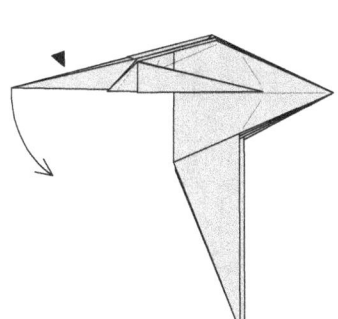

26. Reverse fold the flap down, leaving two layers at the front and one in the back.

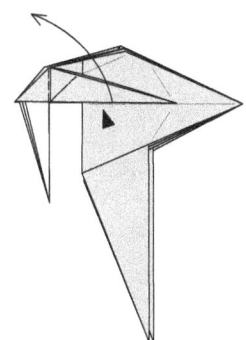

27. Squash the flap up.

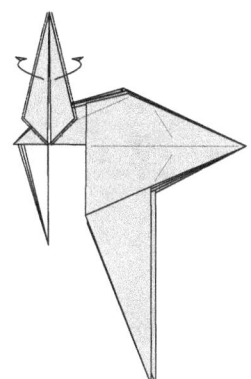

28. Wrap around a single layer at each side.

55

grim reaper

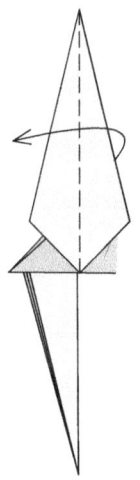
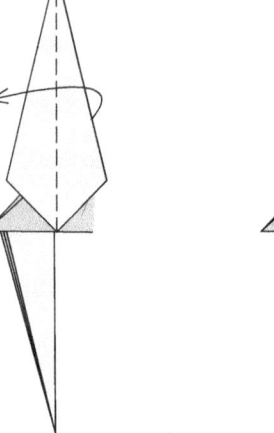
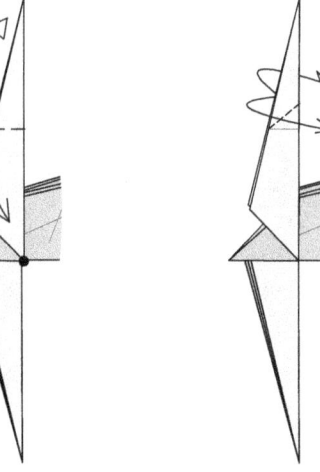
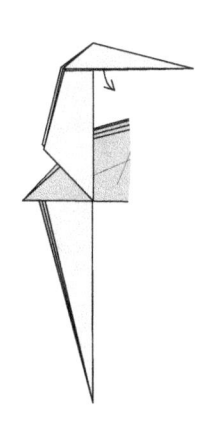

29. Valley fold in half.

30. Precrease in half.

31. Outside reverse fold.

32. Pull out a single layer.

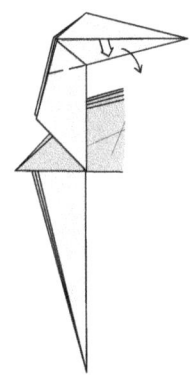
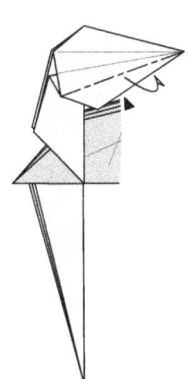
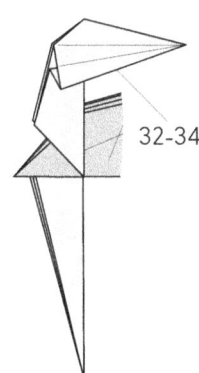
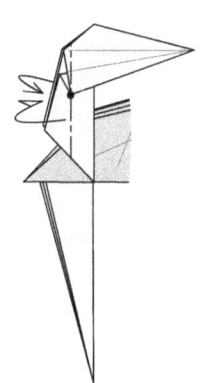

33. Spread apart the trapped pleat and flatten.

34. Reverse fold the edge.

35. Repeat steps 32-34 behind.

36. Mountain fold the sides, aligning with the dotted corner.

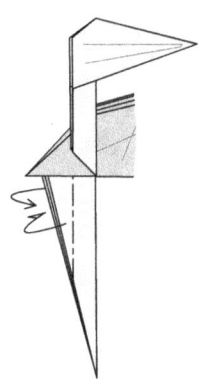
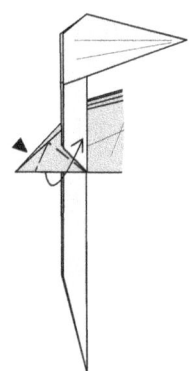
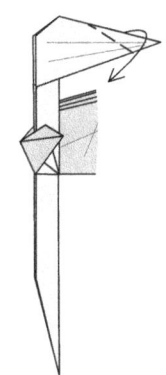
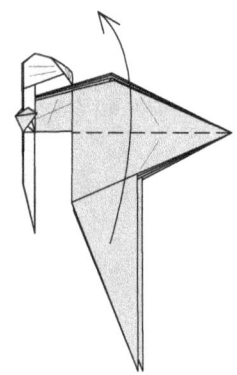

37. Mountain fold the sides below to match the flap above.

38. Squash the corner.

39. Curl the tip over.

40. Swing up one flap.

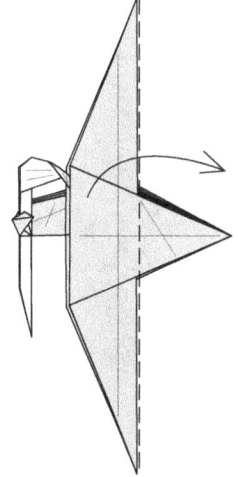

41. Swing over one flap.

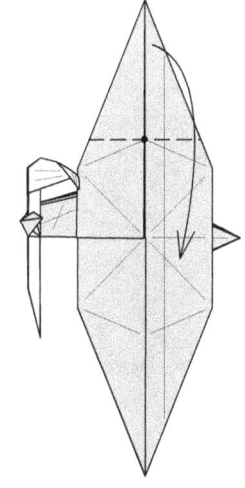

42. Valley fold the flap through the dotted intersection of creases.

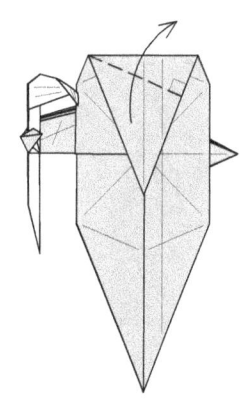

43. Valley fold up, keeping the edges aligned.

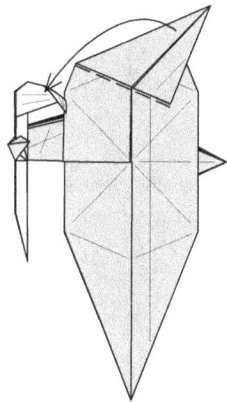

44. Unfold the last step.

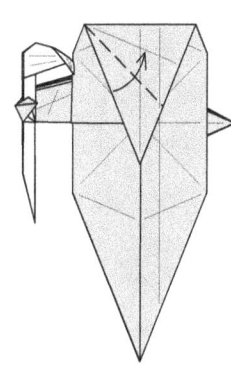

45. Valley fold towards the crease.

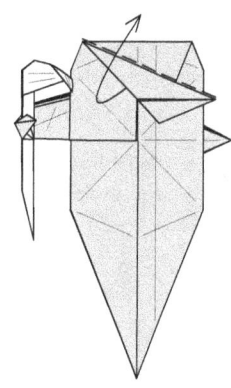

46. Pull around a single layer and flatten.

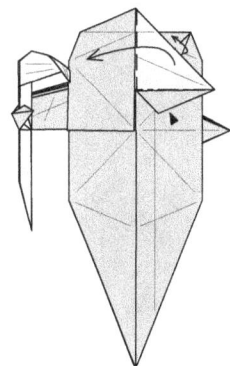

47. Squash the center flap over.

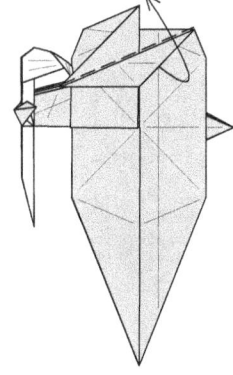

48. Pull around a single layer and flatten.

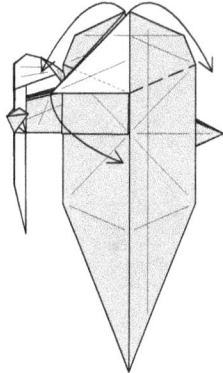

49. Spread open the top flaps and flatten.

grim reaper

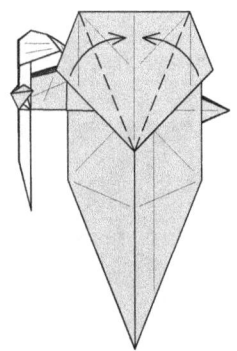 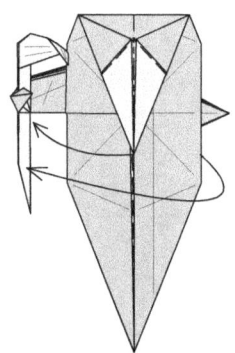 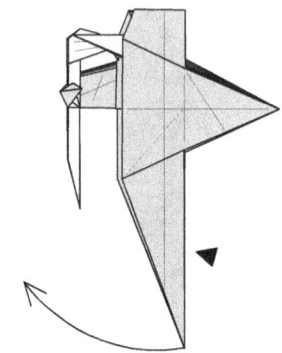

50. Valley fold the sides to the center.

51. Valley fold in half while reverse folding the small flap.

52. Reverse fold the flap.

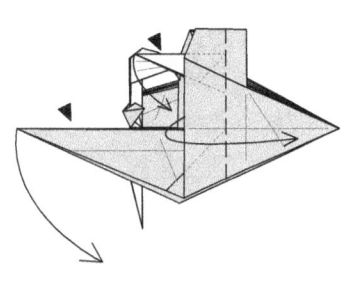 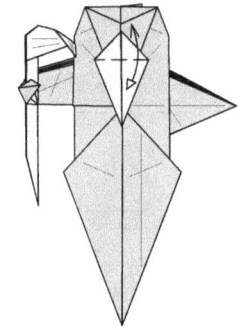 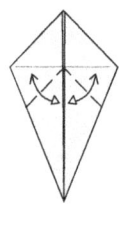

53. Valley fold along the existing crease while squash folding the two flaps down.

54. Precrease the top flap.

55. Precrease the same flap along the angle bisectors.

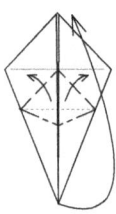 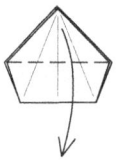 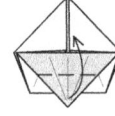

56. Squash fold the flap.

57. Valley fold down.

58. Valley fold slightly beyond the edge.

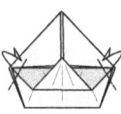 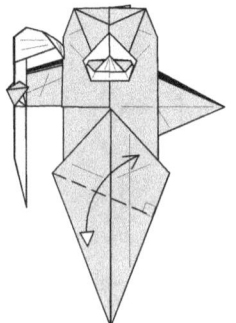 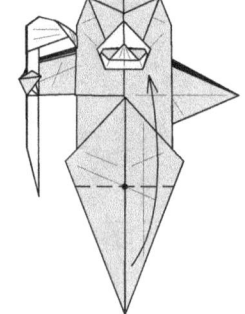

59. Mountain fold the corners in slightly.

60. Precrease the top flap.

61. Valley fold through the dotted intersection of creases.

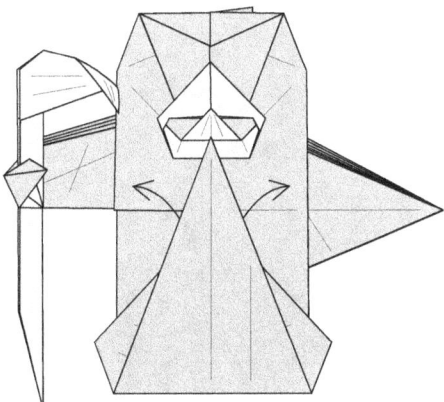

62. Slide out the side layers and flatten, leaving the sides at a slight angle.

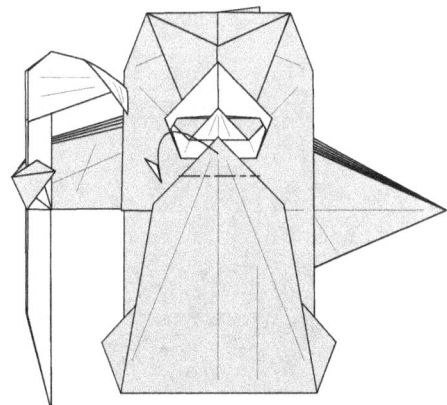

63. Mountain fold the corner.

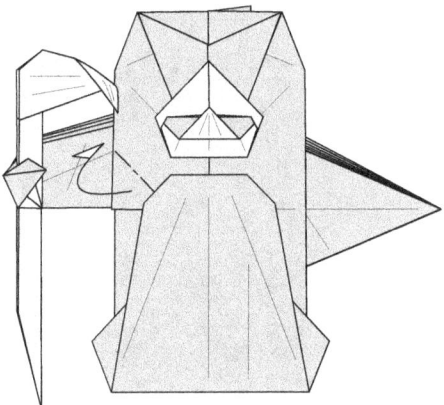

64. Mountain fold the corner.

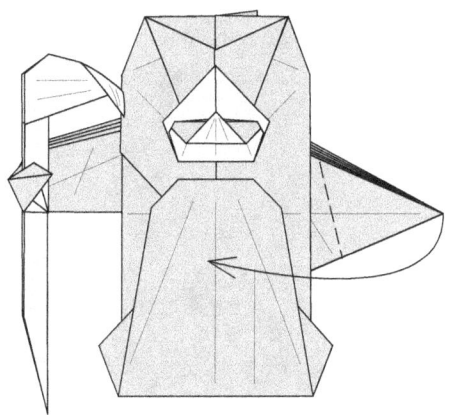

65. Valley fold the flap over.

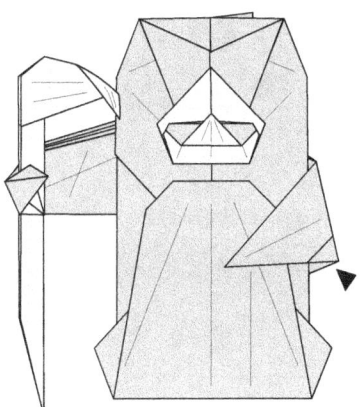

66. Reverse fold the corner.

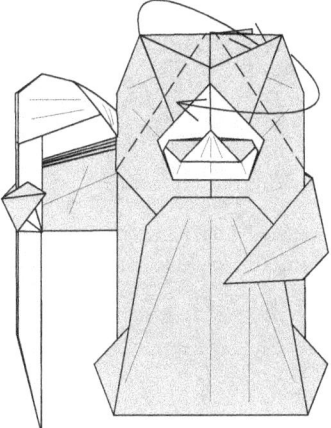

67. Tuck the corner of one flap into the pocket of the other, leaving the sides curved.

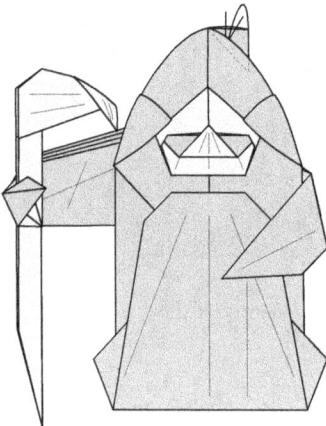
68. Tuck the protruding corner inside.

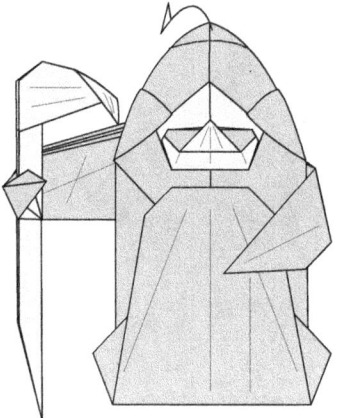
69. Mountain fold the tip to lock the sides together.

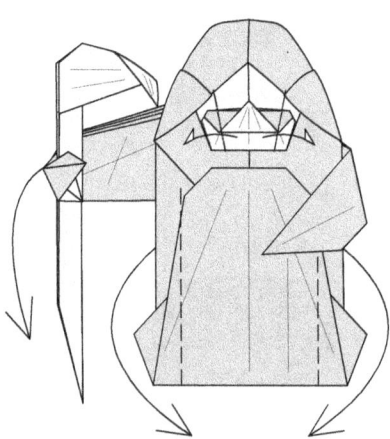
70. Round the sides and the head. Bring the arm with the scythe forward slightly so the model will stand.

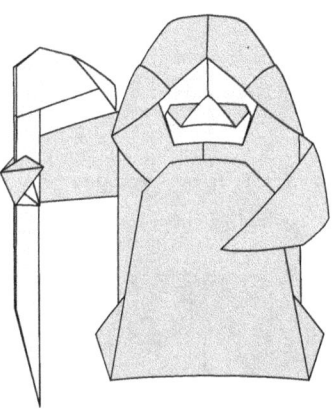
71. Completed *Grim Reaper*.

Japanese Monster

The Japanese are masters of infusing everything with cuteness, and they have managed to make several adorable monsters. A particularly popular one became the mascot for a public broadcasting company, and had its likeness plastered on a wide range of products once it was embraced in the West. This origami *Japanese Monster* is based on this icon, and like the original sports a gape-mouthed, sawtooth adorned set of jaws that eclipses its face and body. Its bark is louder than its bite, especially since that expression is fixed.

japanese monster

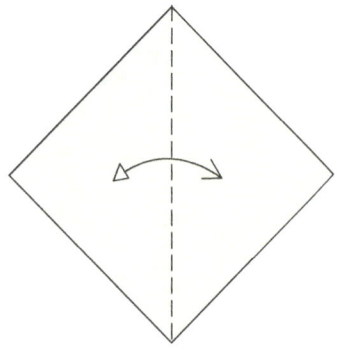

1. Precrease along the diagonal.

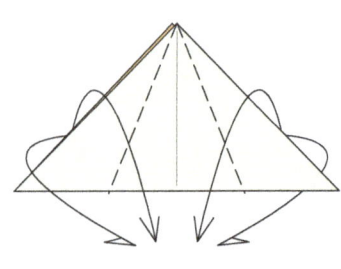

2. Mountain fold.

3. Outside reverse fold.

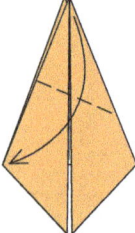

4. Valley fold to the corner.

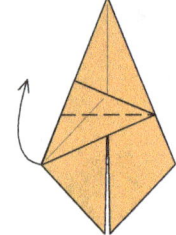

5. Valley fold up.

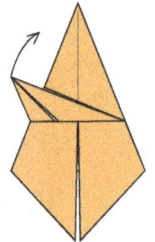

6. Unfold the pleat.

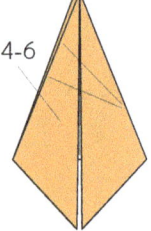

7. Repeat steps 4-6 in mirror image.

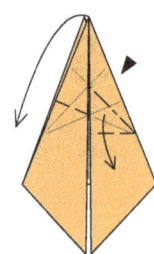

8. Squash fold.

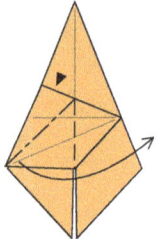

9. Squash fold.

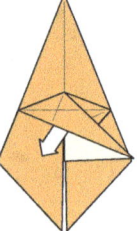

10. Pull out a single layer and flatten.

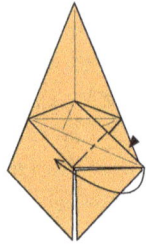

11. Reverse fold.

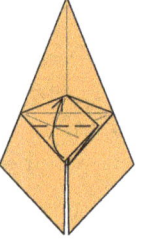

12. Valley fold the top flap up.

japanese monster

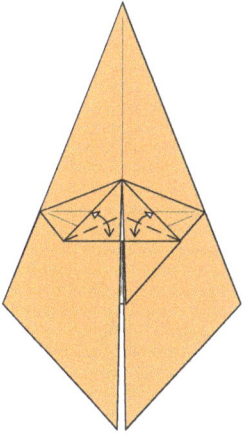

13. Precrease along the angle bisectors.

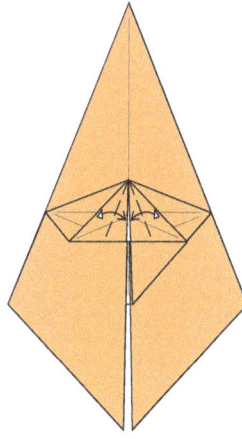

14. Precrease along the angle bisectors.

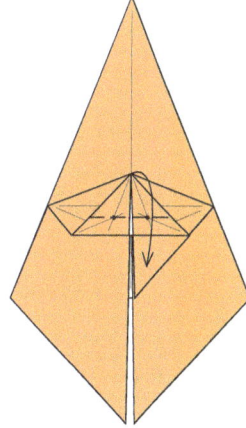

15. Valley fold through the dotted intersections.

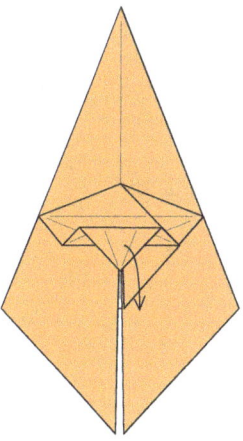

16. Unfold the pleat.

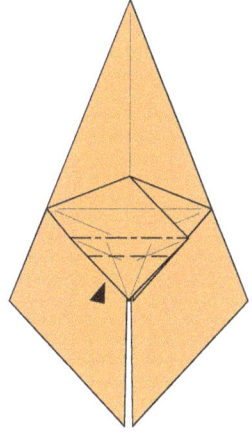

17. Sink the flap in and then out.

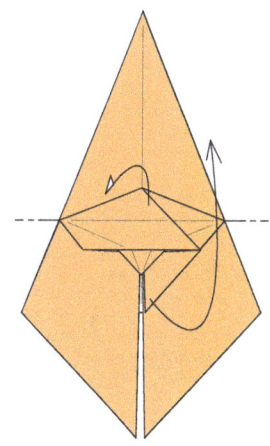

18. Flip the cluster of flaps up.

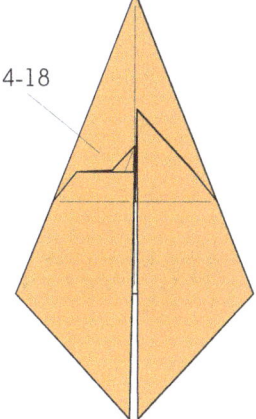

4-18

19. Repeat steps 4-18 behind.

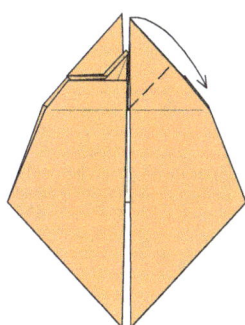

20. Valley fold down.

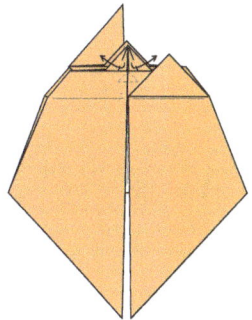

21. Swivel the top layers outwards.

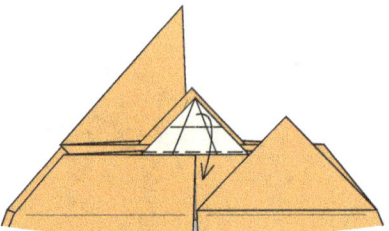

22. Pleat the flap down.

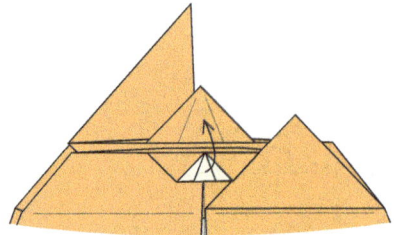

23. Unfold the pleat.

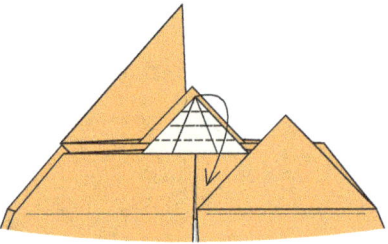

24. Form a new pleat by inserting valley folds between the existing creases.

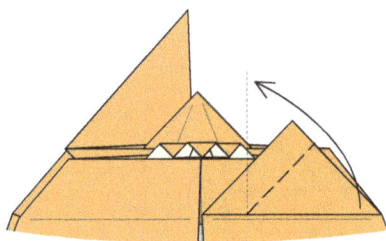

25. Valley fold a small amount past the corner of the triangle.

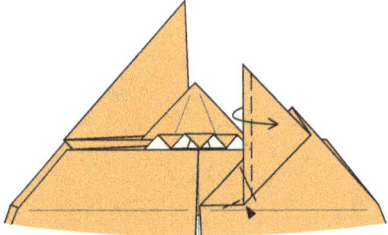

26. Valley fold to align with the hidden triangle corner.

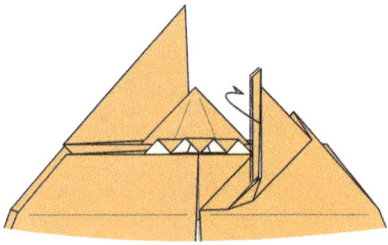

27. Wrap around a single layer.

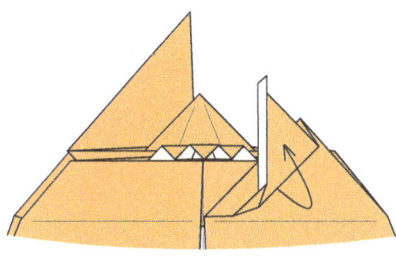
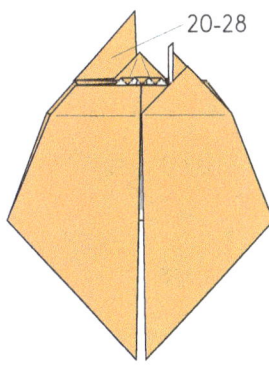

28. Wrap around a single layer (closed reverse fold).

29. Repeat steps 20-28 behind.

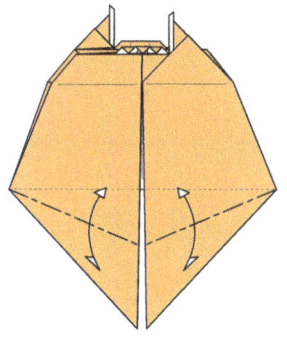
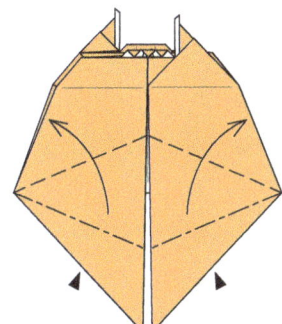
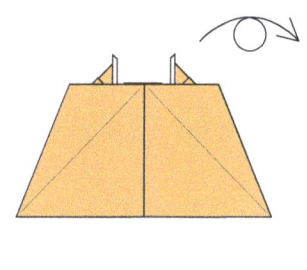

30. Precrease along the angle bisectors using the imaginary line.

31. Squash fold the flaps.

32. Turn over.

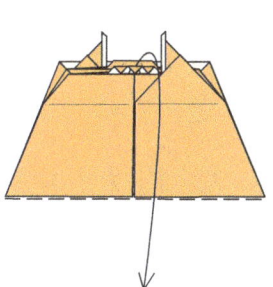
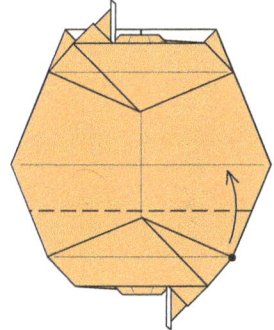
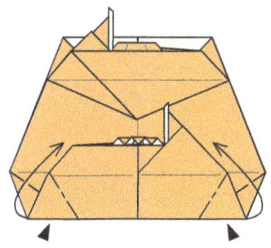

33. Swing down along the center.

34. Valley fold up so the dotted corner hits the crease.

35. Reverse fold the sides.

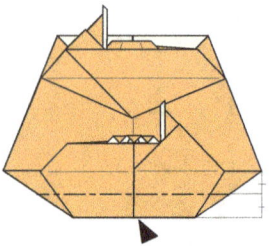

36. Sink the bottom halfway.

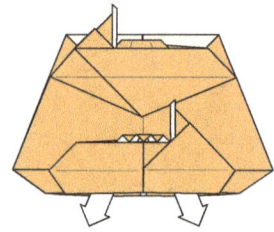

37. Unsink a single layer at each side.

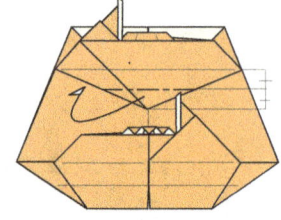

38. Mountain fold the corner inside.

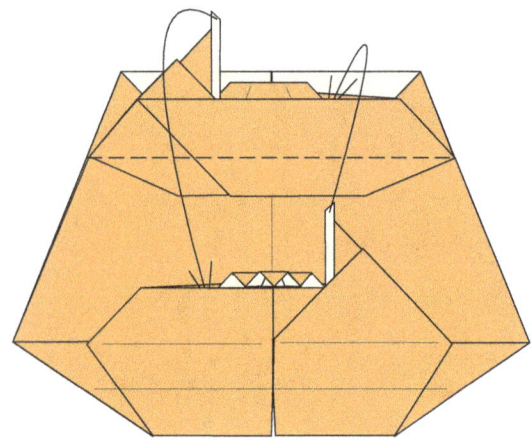

39. Valley fold down, allowing the indicated flaps to get tucked into the pockets.

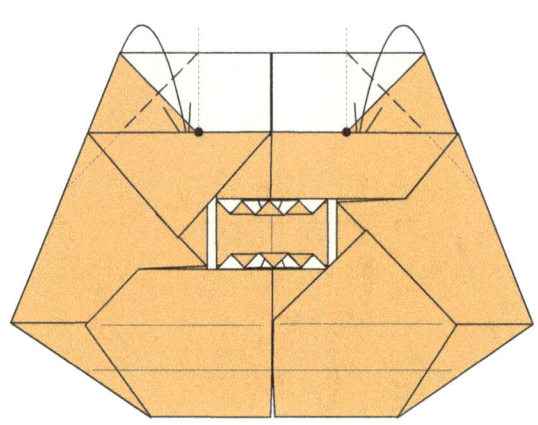

40. Valley fold the back layer so it hits the dotted intersection.

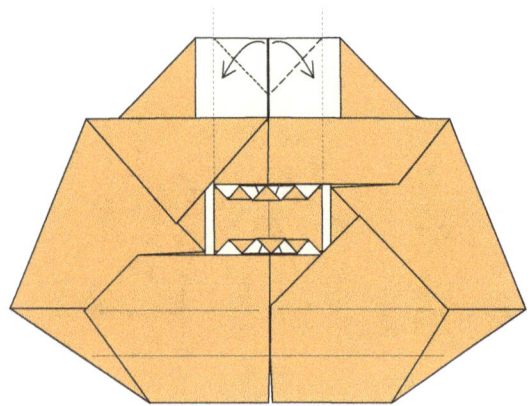

41. Valley fold the corners to align with the imaginary reference.

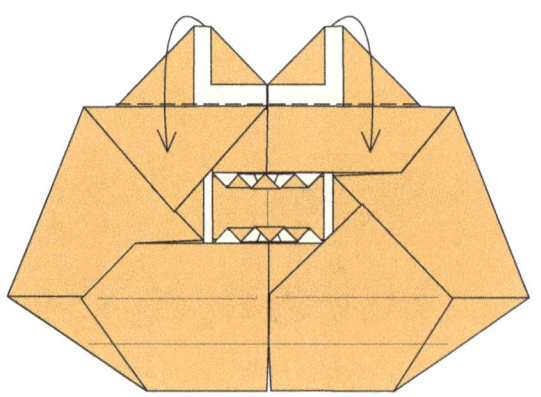

42. Valley fold the flaps down.

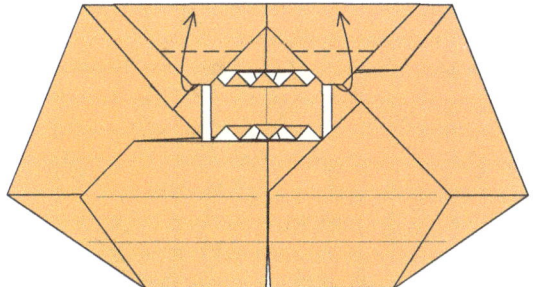

43. Valley fold the flaps up. This will determine the baseline of the eyes.

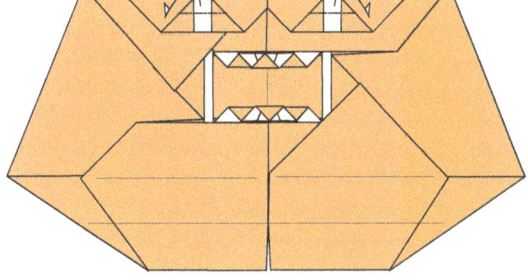

44. Mountain fold the edges inside to square off the eyes.

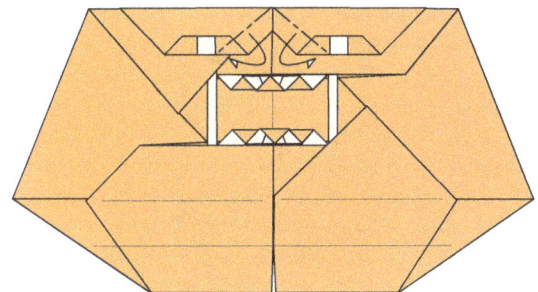

45. Mountain fold the side edges inside.

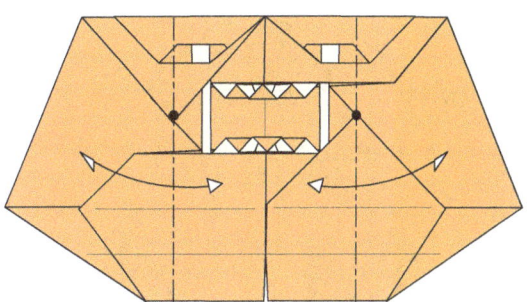

46. Precrease with mountain folds through the dotted intersections.

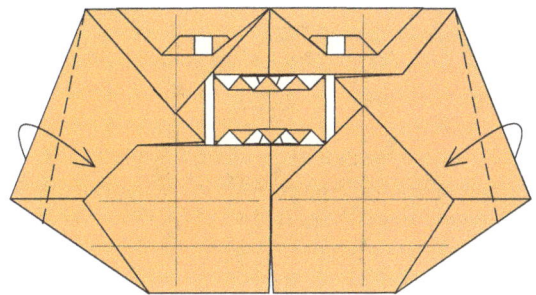

47. Valley fold so the side edges lie straight.

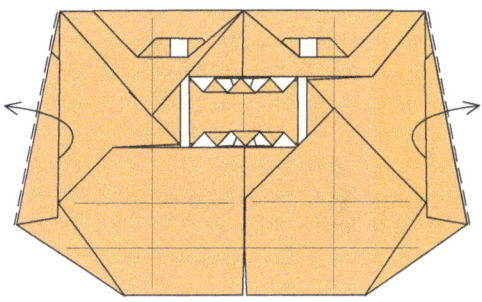

48. Unfold.

japanese monster

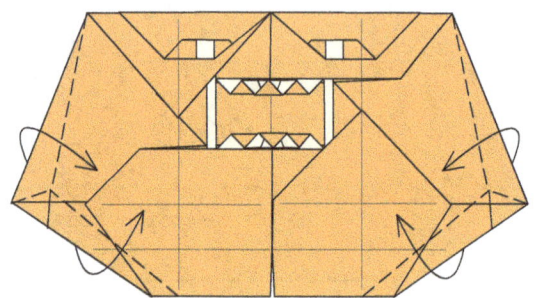

49. Rabbit ear the sides.

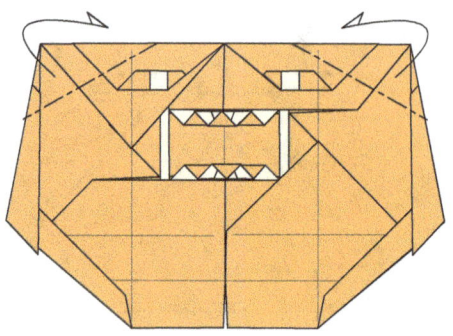

50. Mountain fold the corners (the angle is to taste).

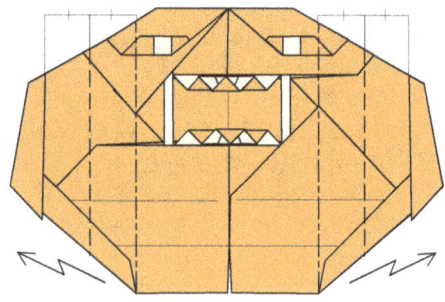

51. Pleat the sides.

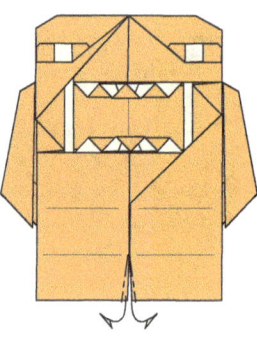

52. Mountain fold the inner edges in slightly.

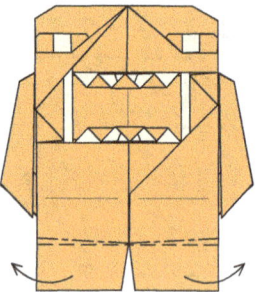

53. Pleat the legs outwards.

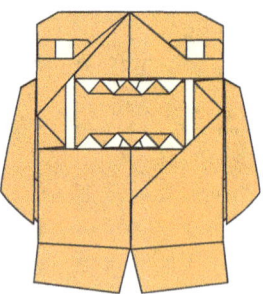

54. Completed *Japanese Monster*.

Hand in the Box

We all love presents, and an inviting gift box will surely send our expectations high. Anyone would be blindsided into shock if opening the lid revealed a disembodied hand. It would be even more frightening if only its bones remained and was animated by a protruding arm. This origami *Hand in the Box* depicts such a horror, sporting a limb that is curiously larger than the sides that contain it.

hand in the box

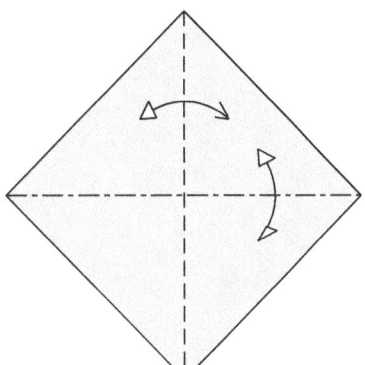

1. Precrease with both valley and mountain folds.

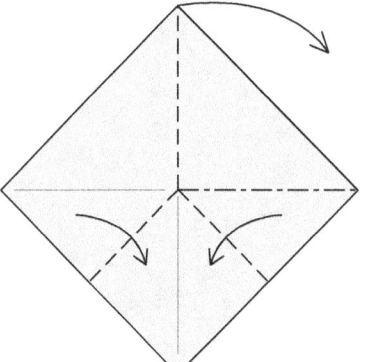

2. Rabbit ear.

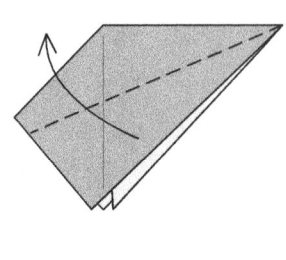

3. Valley fold along the angle bisector.

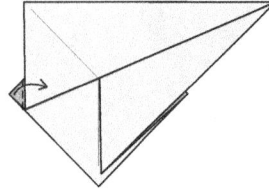

4. Valley fold over the protruding corner.

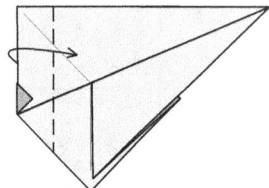

5. Valley fold to the center.

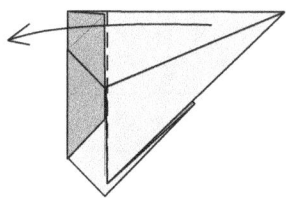

6. Valley fold the large flap over.

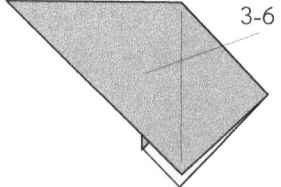

7. Repeat steps 3-6 in mirror image.

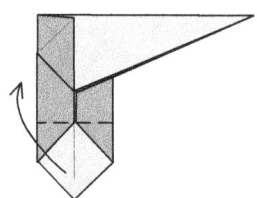

8. Lightly valley fold up.

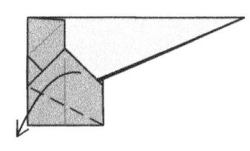

9. Lightly valley fold down.

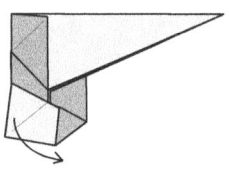

10. Unfold the pleat.

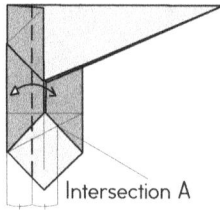

11. Precrease over to intersection A.

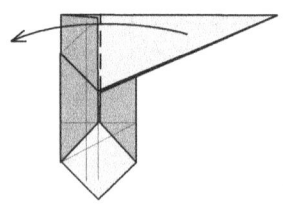

12. Swing over the center flap.

hand in the box

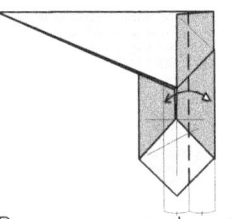

13. Precrease over to the existing crease.

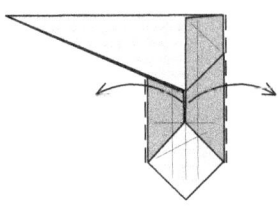

14. Swing the side flaps outwards.

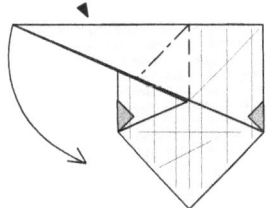

15. Squash the center flap.

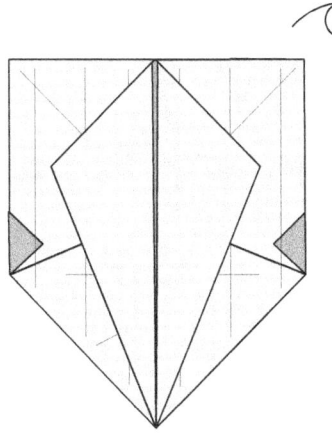

16. Turn over.

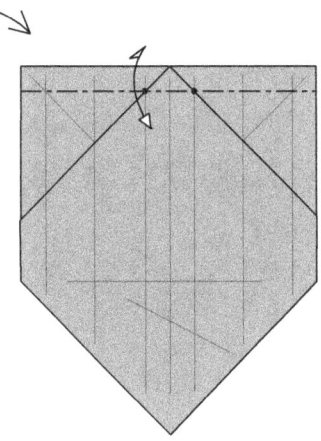

17. Precrease through the dotted intersections of creases.

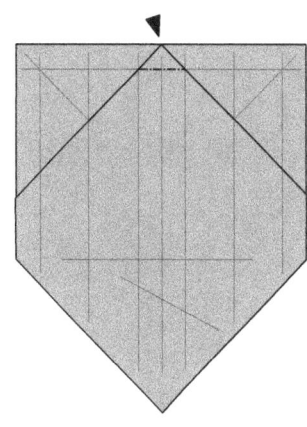

18. Sink the trapped point. You will have to open up the model to do this.

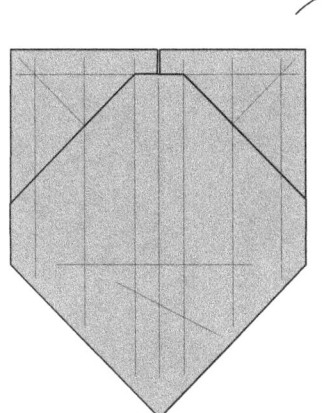

19. Turn over.

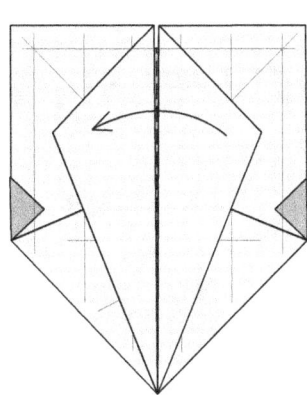

20. Swing over the large flap.

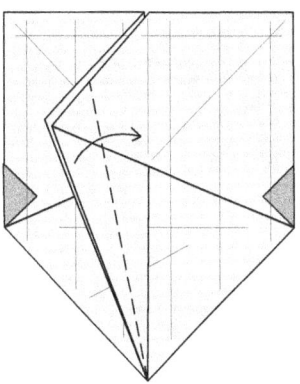

21. Valley fold along the angle bisector.

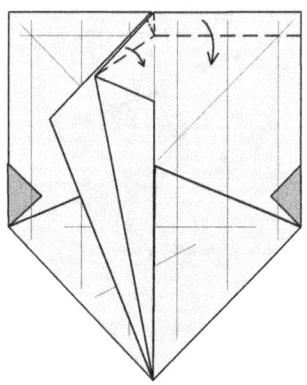

22. Valley fold along the crease, allowing a pleat to form.

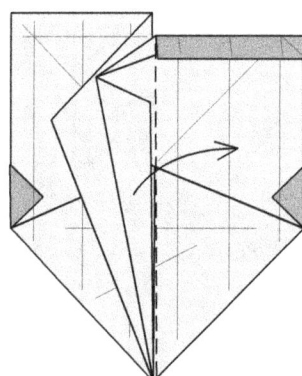

23. Open out the pleat.

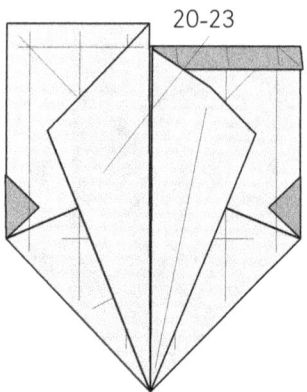

24. Repeat steps 20-23 in mirror image.

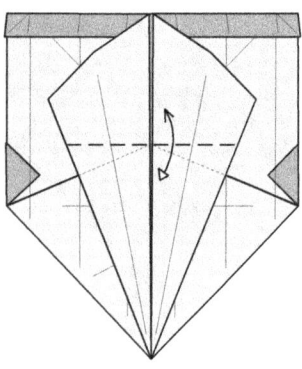

25. Precrease lightly above the hidden edges.

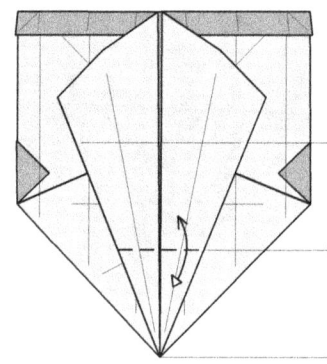

26. Precrease again.

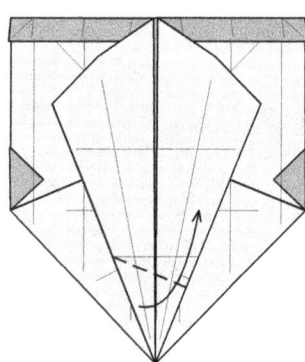

27. Valley fold over.

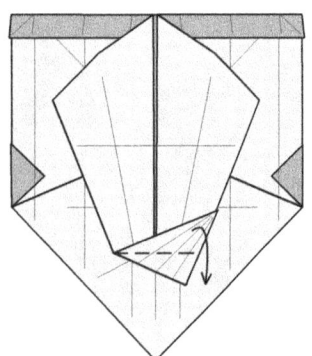

28. Valley fold down.

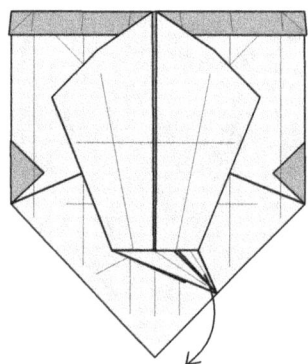

29. Unfold the pleat.

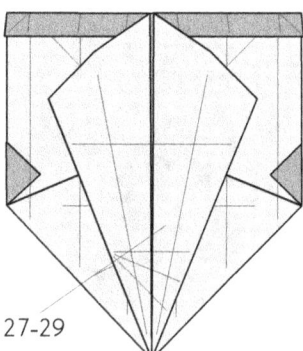

30. Repeat steps 27-29 in mirror image.

hand in the box

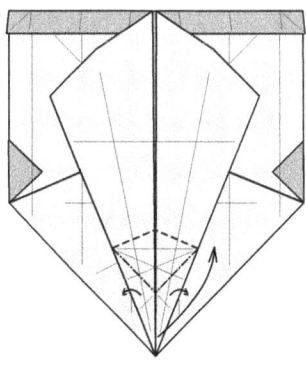

31. Open out the inner edges, and squash fold flat.

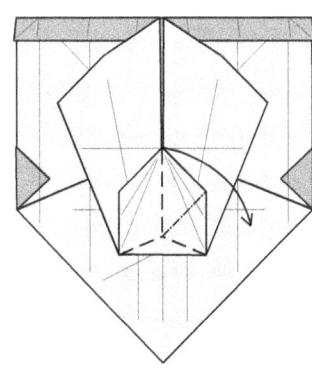

32. Rabbit ear the flap down.

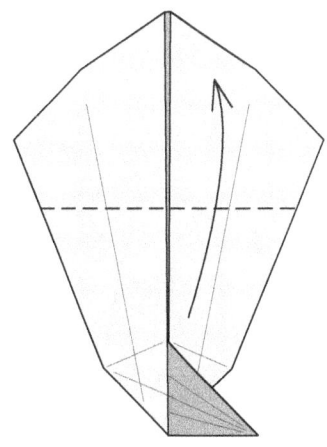

33. Lightly valley fold up.

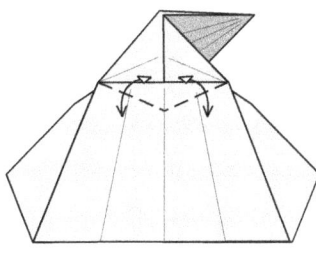

34. Precrease the top edge down as far as possible.

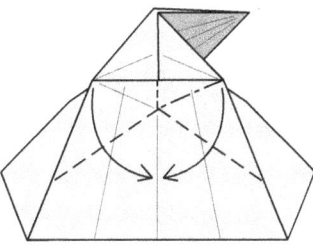

35. Rabbit ear the top section.

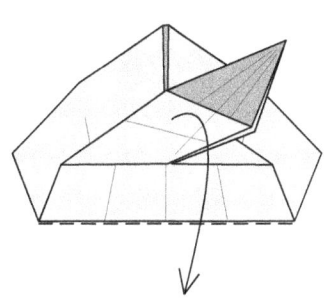

36. Swing the top section down.

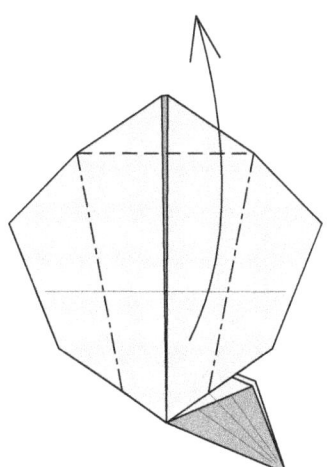

37. Petal fold upwards.

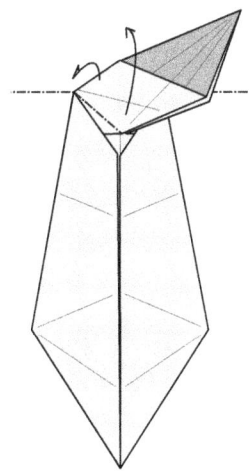

38. Flip the top section, while releasing the trapped layers.

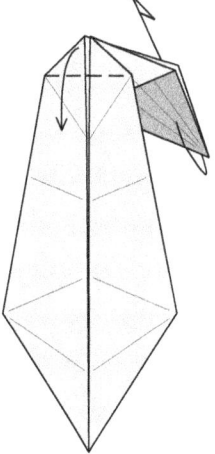

39. Flip back up.

73

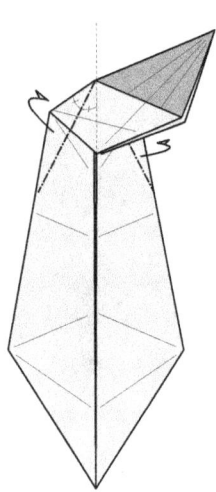

40. Mountain fold the sides along the angle bisectors.

41. Spread apart the sides, allowing squashes to form.

42. Pleat the top section down.

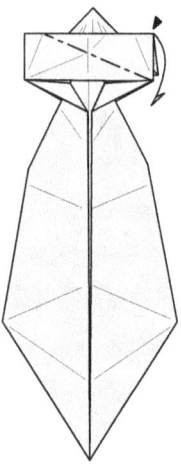
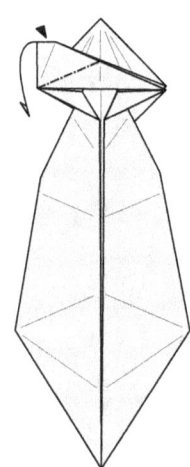
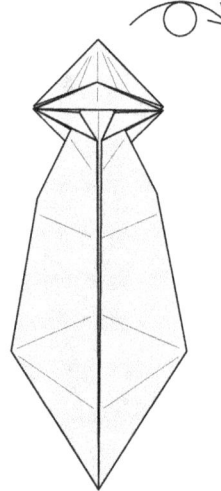

43. Reverse fold, using the existing crease as a guide.

44. Form a closed reverse fold at the other side.

45. Turn over.

hand in the box

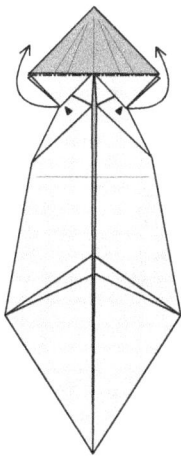

46. Reverse fold the two corners upwards.

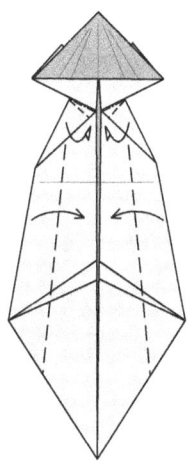

47. Valley fold the sides to the center, swiveling in the excess paper.

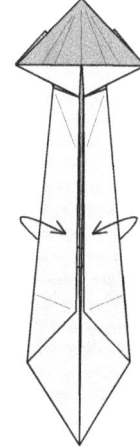

48. Wrap a layer around at each side. Part of the wrapped area is hidden.

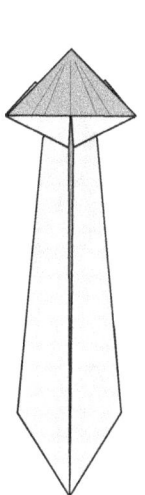

49. Turn over.

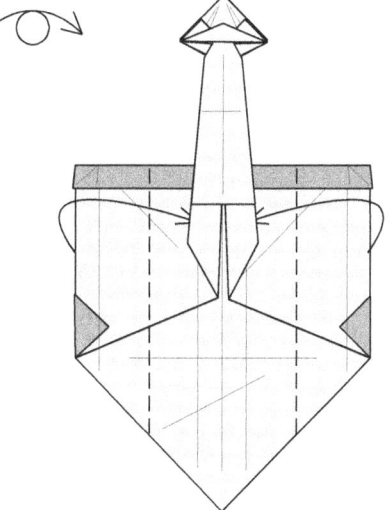

50. Valley fold the flaps to the center, tucking them under.

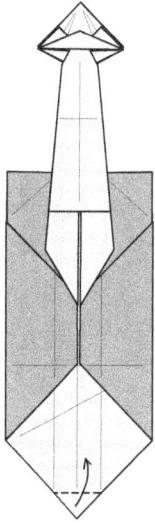

51. Valley fold the bottom corner up where it hits the crease lines.

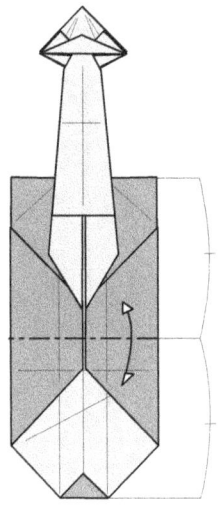
52. Precrease in half with a mountain fold.

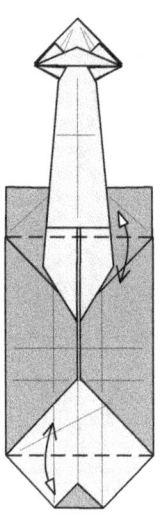
53. Precrease where indicated.

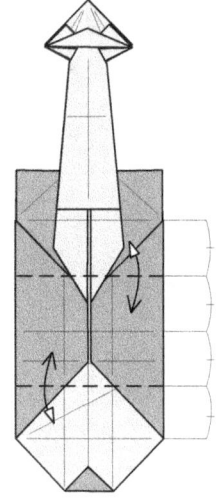
54. Precrease at the indicated divisions.

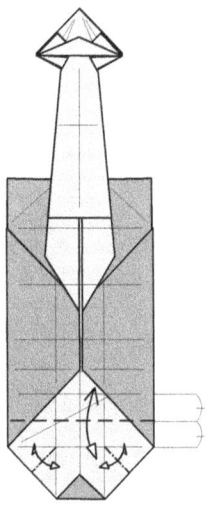
55. Add more precreases.

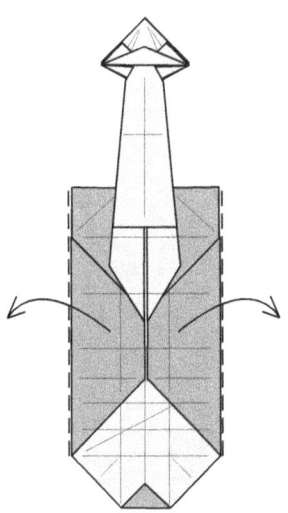
56. Open out the sides again.

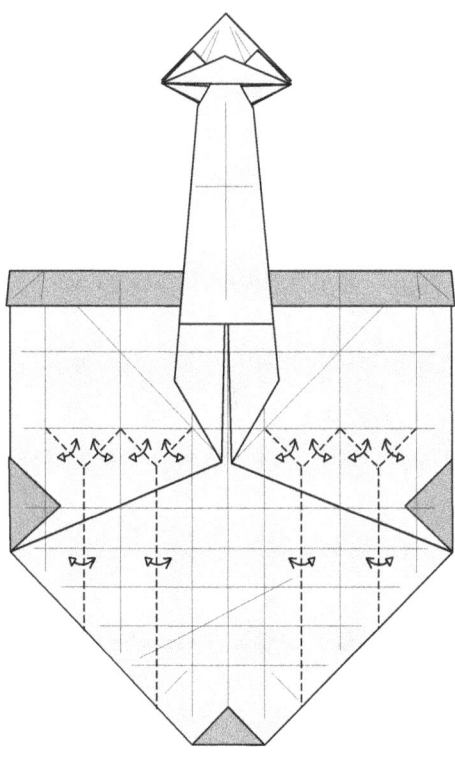

57. Form the indicated precreases with valley folds.

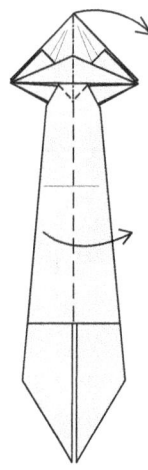

58. Valley fold in half while reverse folding.

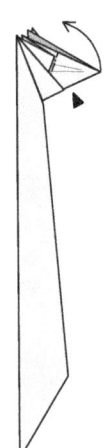

59. Reverse fold the center flap.

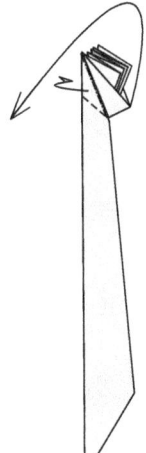

60. Crimp downwards, tucking into the inside pockets.

61. Reverse fold the four corners.

hand in the box

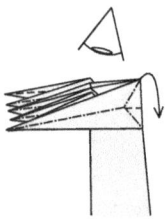 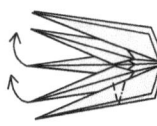 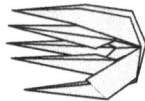

62. Rabbit ear the outer fingers, and double rabbit ear the inner fingers.

63. Pleat the thumb, and group the remaining fingers together.

64. Completed hand. You can curl and shape to taste.

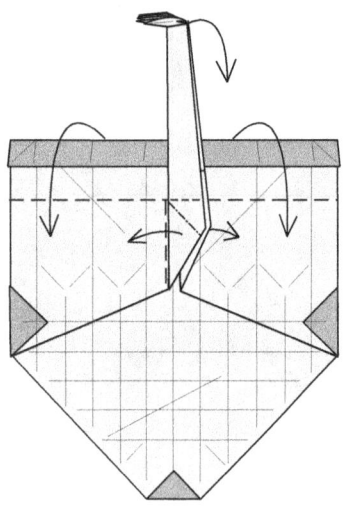 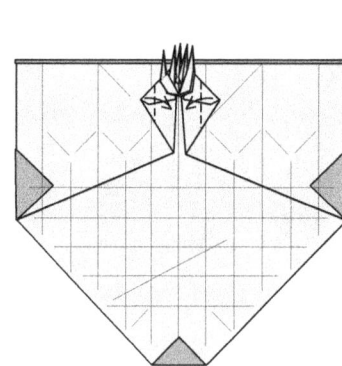 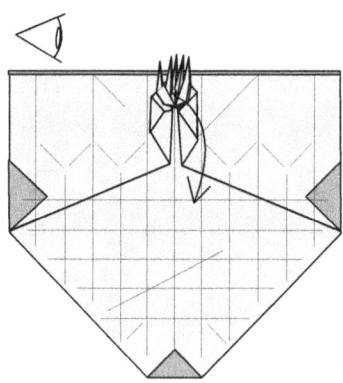

65. Valley fold the side up at 90°, while squashing the base of the arm.

66. Valley fold the corners inwards.

67. Pull the arm away from the face of the box.

 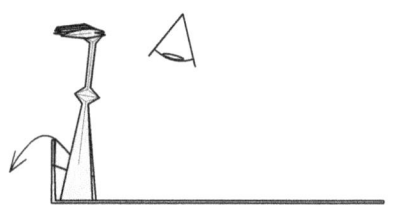

68. View from step 30. Double rabbit ear the arm.

69. Pull the front edge down, allowing the base to unfold temporarily.

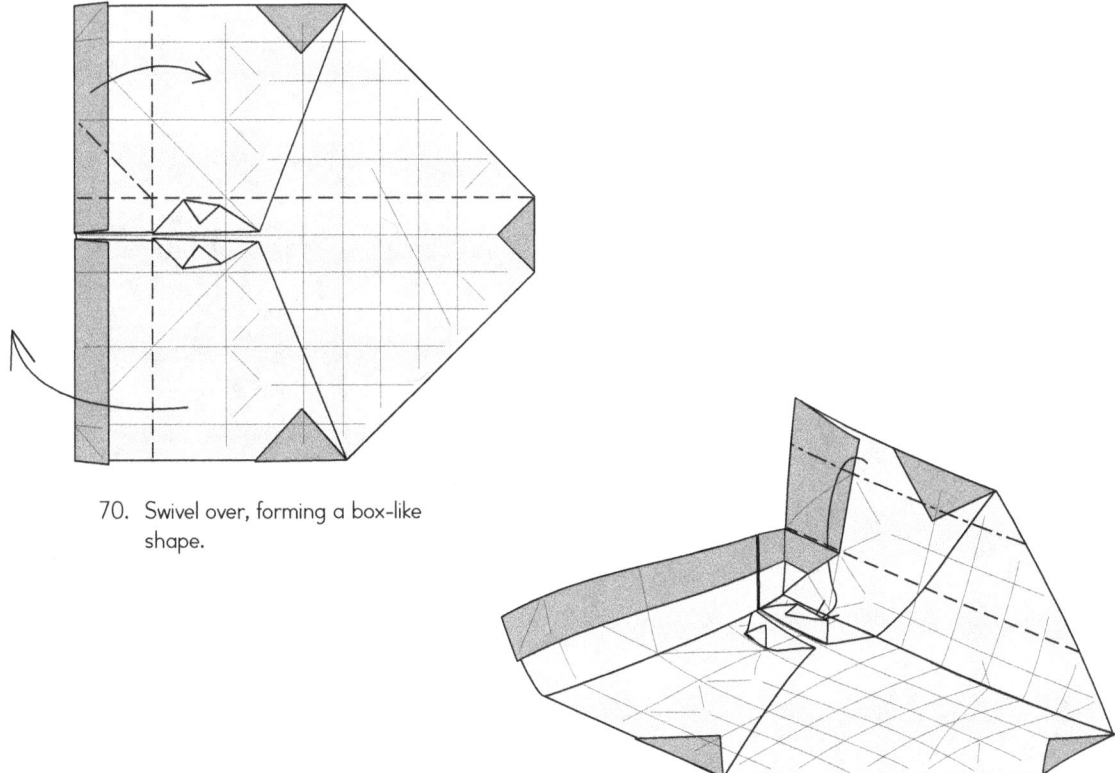

70. Swivel over, forming a box-like shape.

71. Tuck the hem under the flap.

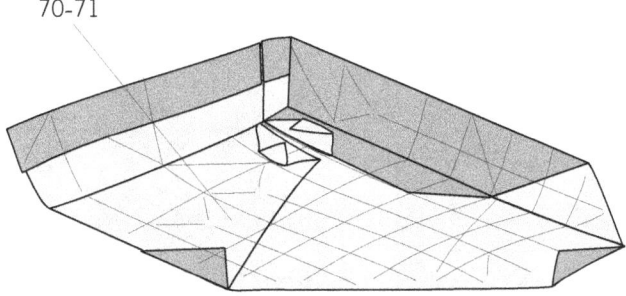

70-71

72. Repeat steps 70-71 on the other side.

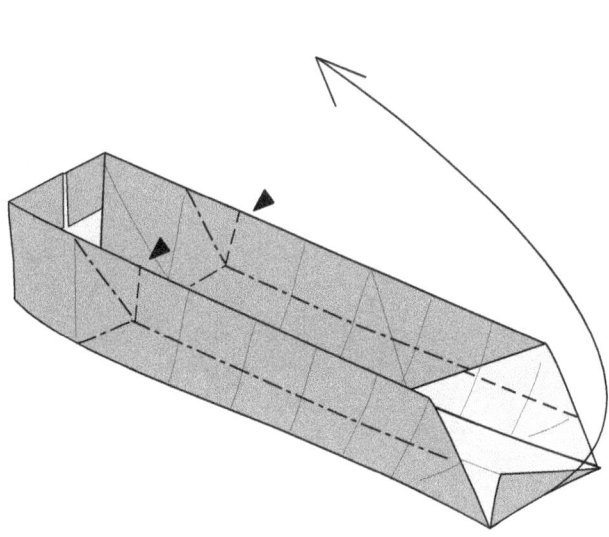

73. Double rabbit ear both sides, distributing the layers as evenly as possible.

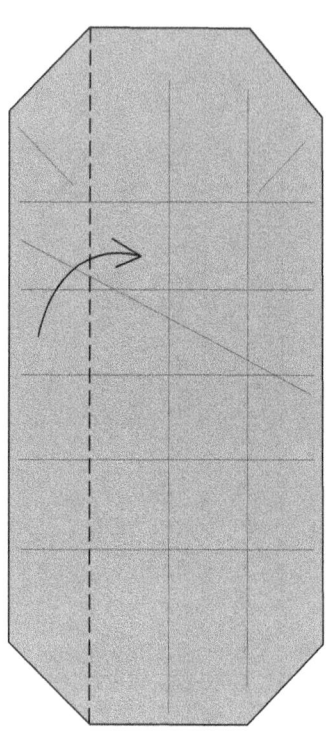

74. Valley fold to the center.

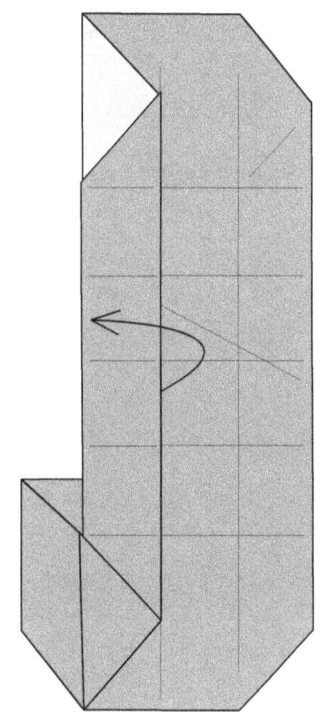

75. Pull the single layer to the surface.

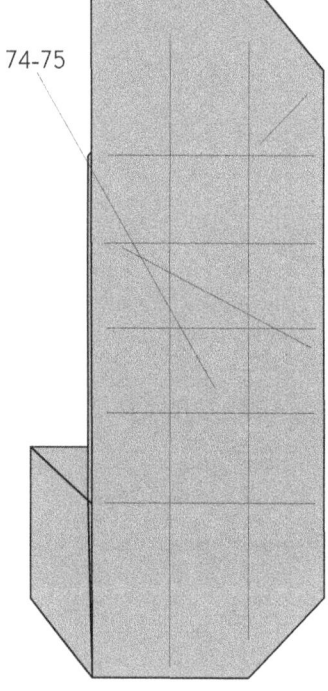

76. Repeat 74-75 on the other side.

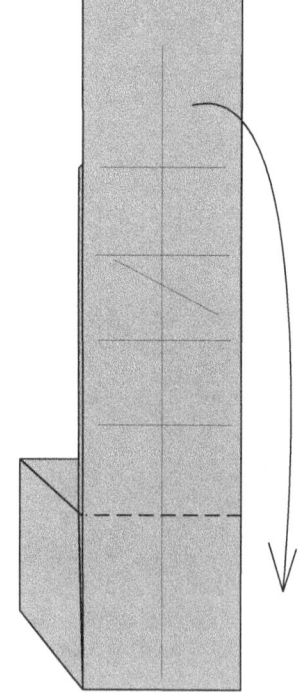

77. Valley fold down.

hand in the box

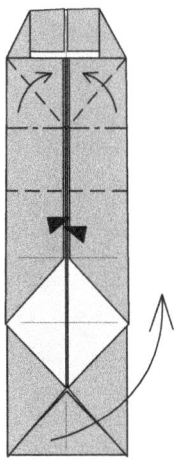 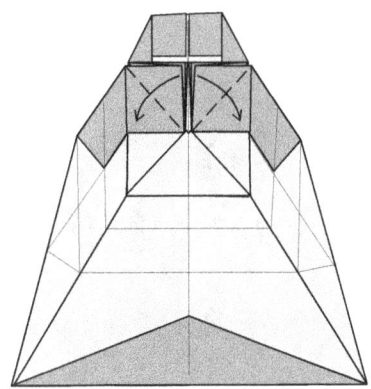 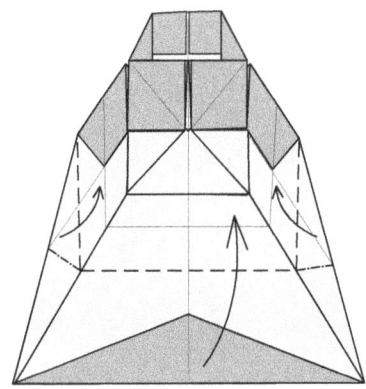

78. Push the center edges out flat, while swiveling at the top.

79. Valley fold the corners down.

80. Bring the bottom upwards, while forming reverse-folds to lie along the sides.

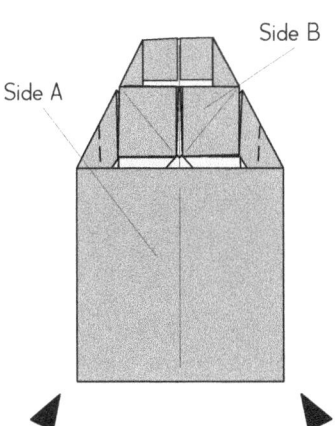 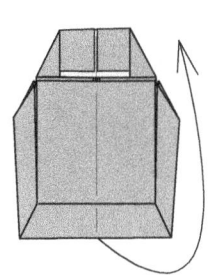 

81. Using the existing creases, invert side A to lie on side B.

82. Pull the set of pleats towards the back of the box. Position the arms, pleats and lid to taste.

83. Completed *Hand in the Box*.

81

Dracula

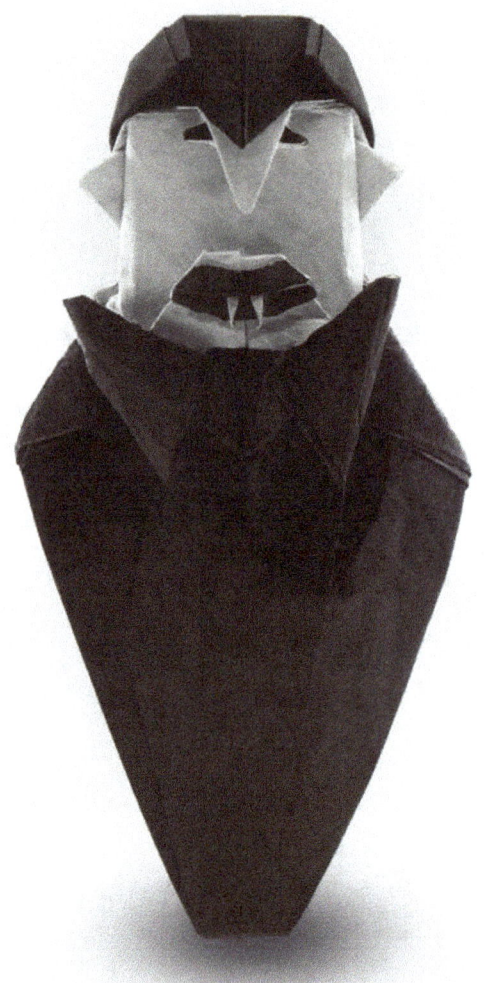

Author Bram Stoker managed to depict perhaps the most iconic monster with his vampire. Sporting a suave refined exterior, The Count preyed on young women and exploited their vulnerability. Later versions of the story would vary the powers he posed, but his ability to literally suck the life out of his victims remained his primal drive. This paper Dracula focuses on depicting his face, outlining the widow's peak hairstyle and pronounced fangs. The body is concealed within its cloak, suggesting there might be some shape-shifting brewing underneath.

dracula

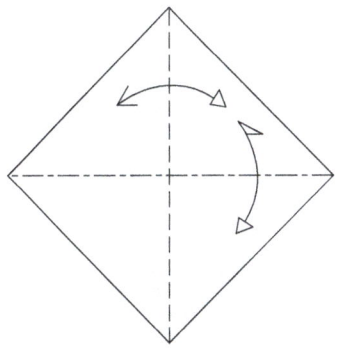

1. Precrease along the diagonals with mountain and valley folds.

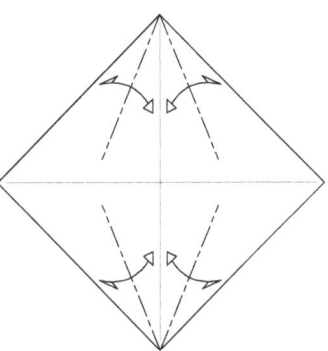

2. Precrease the angle bisectors with mountain folds.

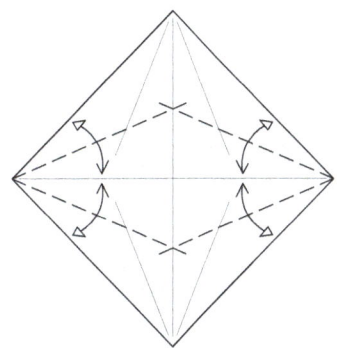

3. Precrease along the angle bisectors, being sure to pass through the center.

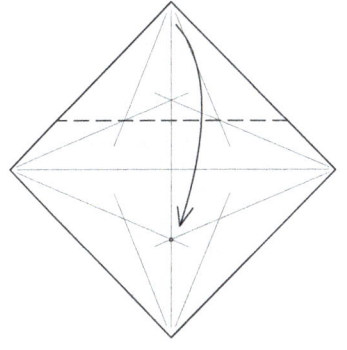

4. Valley fold to the dotted intersection of creases.

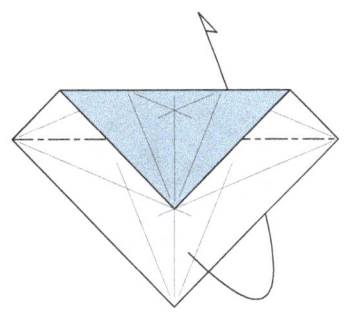

5. Mountain fold.

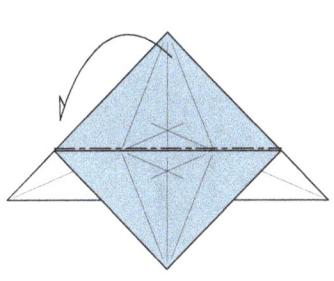

6. Mountain fold, aligning with the folded edge and meeting the bottom corner.

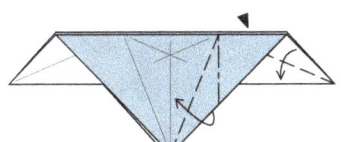

7. Swivel fold.

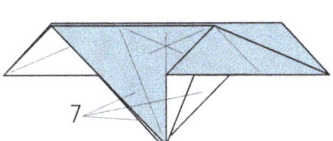

8. Repeat step 7 on the remaining three sides.

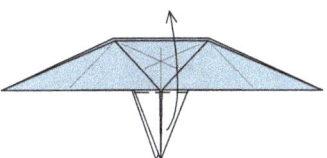

9. Valley fold up.

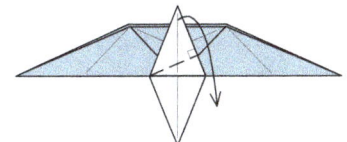

10. Valley fold over, ensuring that the side edges are aligned.

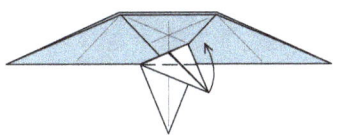

11. Valley fold up.

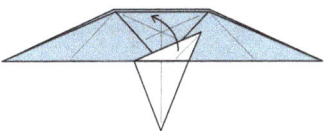

12. Unfold the pleat.

dracula

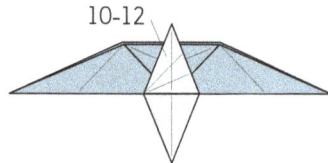

13. Repeat steps 10-12 in mirror image.

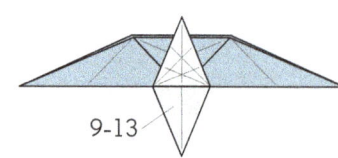

14. Repeat steps 9-13 behind.

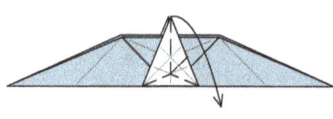

15. Rabbit ear along the existing creases.

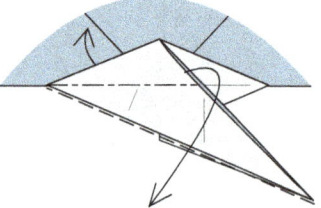

16. Pull out a single trapped layer and flatten.

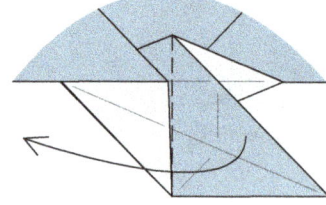

17. Swing over.

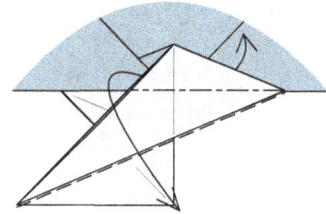

18. Pull out a single trapped layer and flatten.

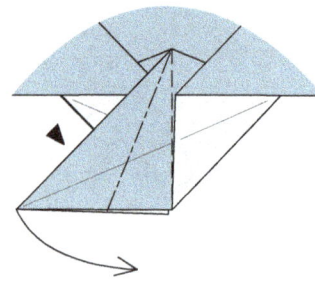

19. Squash fold.

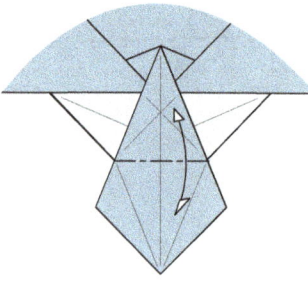

20. Precrease with a mountain fold.

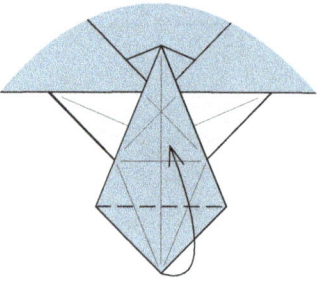

21. Valley fold up.

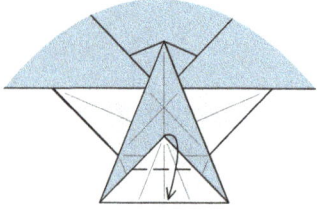

22. Valley fold down.

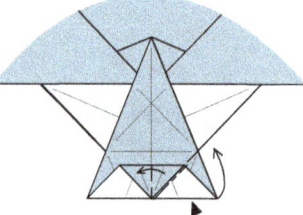

23. Squash fold the corner up.

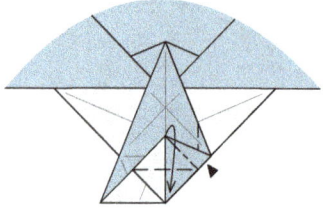

24. Valley fold down, squash folding at the side.

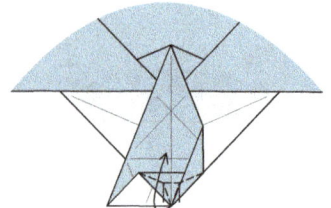

25. Valley fold the flap up while swiveling the sides behind.

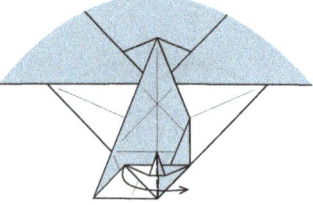

26. Swing the flap over.

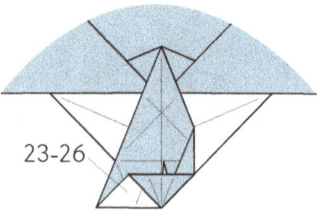

27. Repeat steps 23-26 in mirror image.

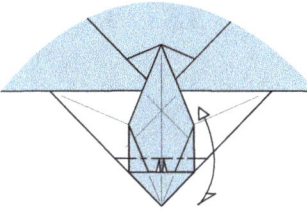
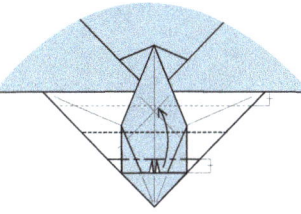
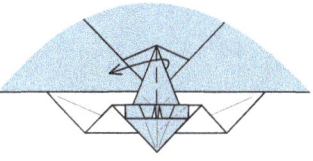

28. Sharpen the crease through all layers.

29. Pleat the crease towards the imaginary reference point.

30. Swivel the flap through.

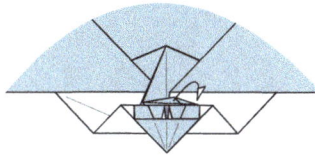
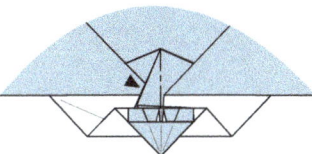
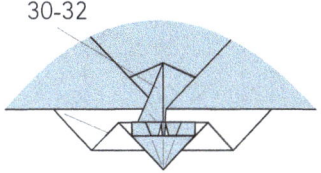

31. Mountain fold the protruding edge inside.

32. Closed sink the flap through.

33. Repeat steps 30-32 in mirror image.

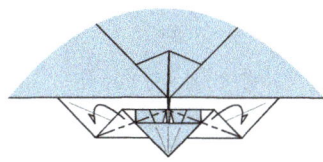
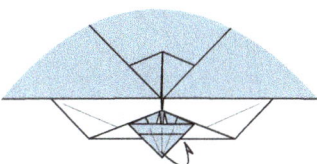
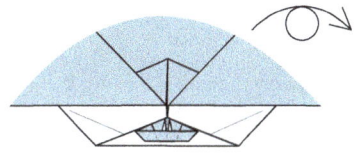

34. Mountain fold the edges behind.

35. Mountain fold the corner in as far as possible.

36. Turn over.

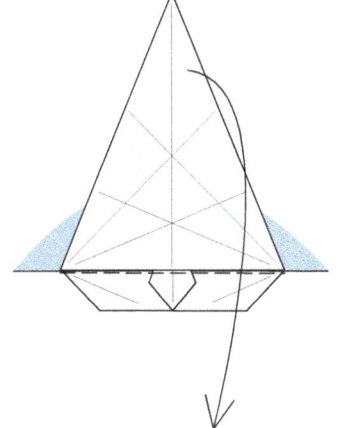
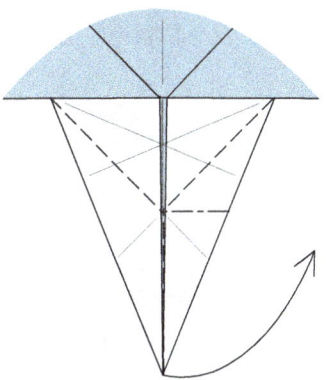
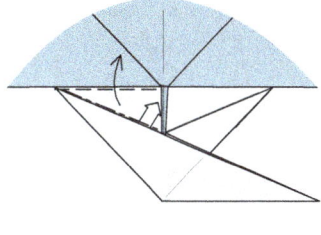

37. Swing the flap down.

38. Rabbit ear along the existing creases.

39. Pull out a single layer and squash flat.

dracula

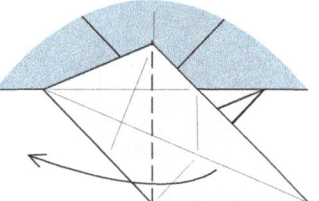

40. Swing the flap over.

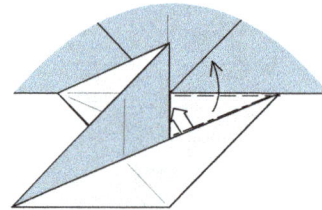

41. Pull out a single layer and squash flat.

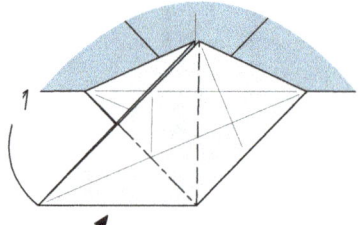

42. Squash the center flap.

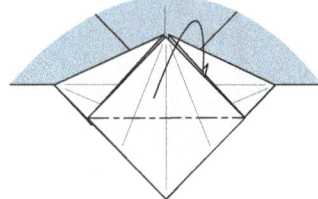

43. Mountain fold the corner inside.

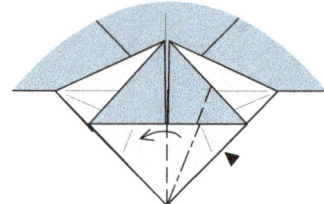

44. Squash fold.

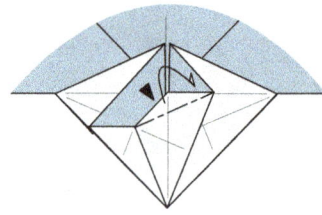

45. Reverse fold the corner.

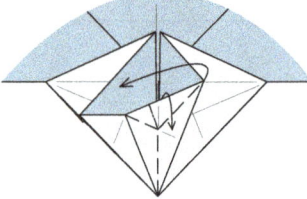

46. Swing over while forming a rabbit ear.

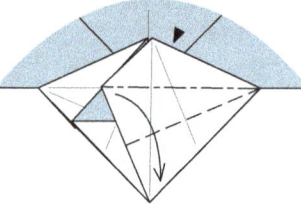

47. Squash the side corner down.

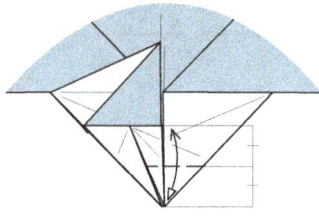

48. Precrease the flap in half.

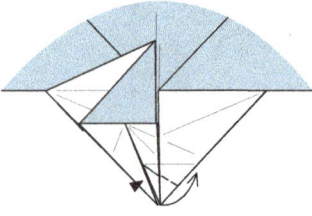

49. Reverse fold, distributing only a single layer at the top.

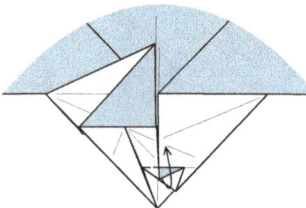

50. Open out the flap.

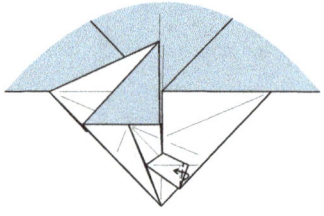

51. Valley fold towards the imaginary reference.

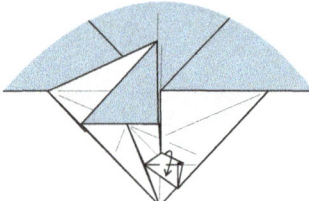

52. Swing the flap back down.

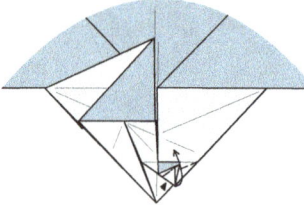

53. Reverse fold, so that a little of the edge can be seen on each side of the flap.

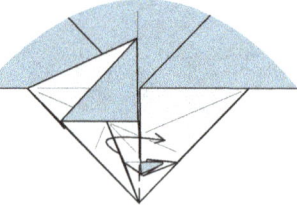

54. Swing over.

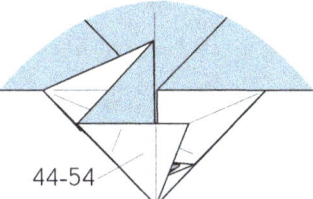
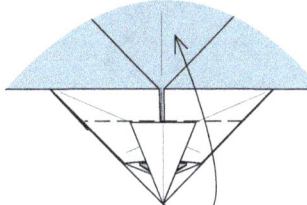
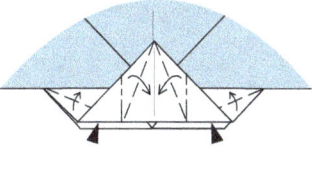

55. Repeat steps 44-54 in mirror image.

56. Valley fold up.

57. Swivel in the sides.

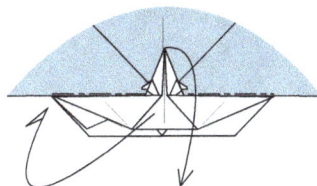
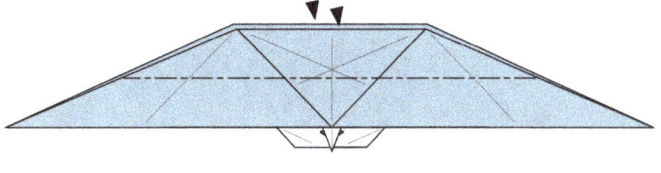

58. Flip the bottom edge inside.

59. Closed sink each flap halfway.

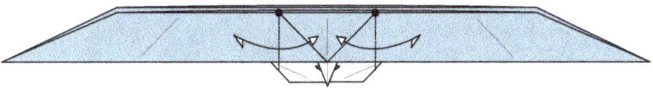

60. Precrease with mountain folds.

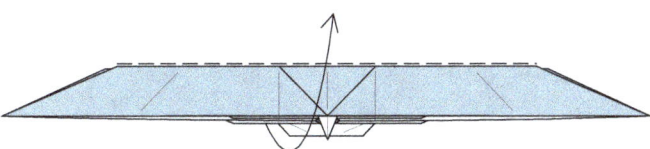

61. Raise the layers to reveal the bottom layer. The sides will not lie flat.

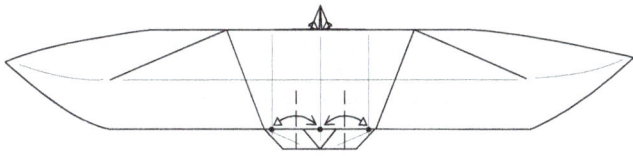

62. Precrease the dotted sections in half.

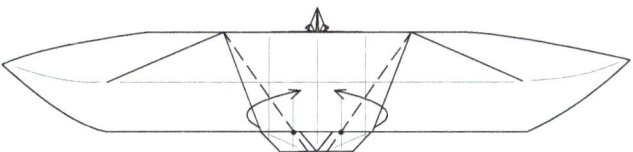

63. Valley fold, being sure to pass through the dotted intersections.

dracula

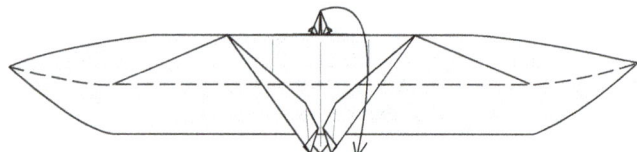

64. Swing the layers back down.

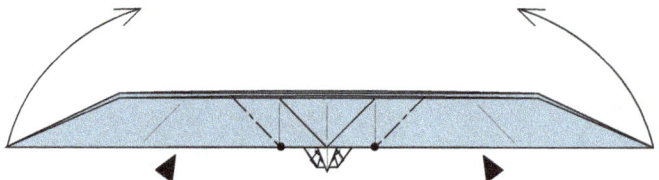

65. Reverse fold the sides up, starting from the dotted intersections.

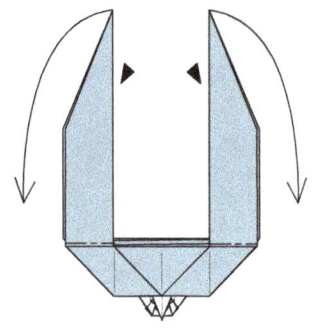

66. Reverse fold the sides down.

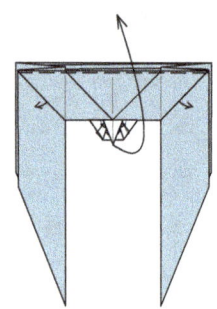

67. Pull the top layer up, releasing the trapped layers at the sides to facilitate this.

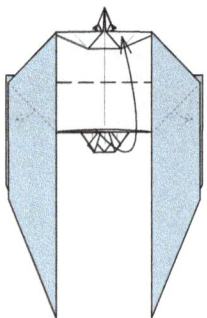

68. Pull the next layer up.

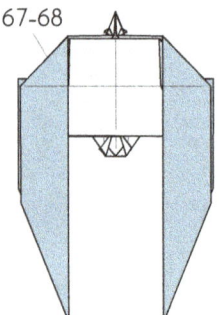

69. Repeat steps 67-68 behind.

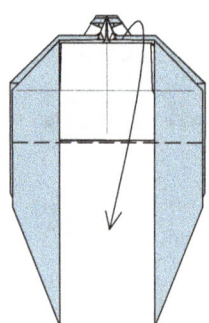

70. Swing down the top section, flattening out the inside.

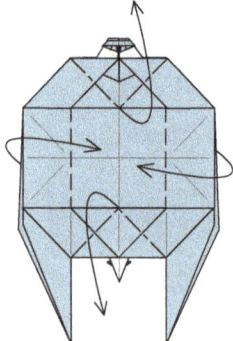

71. Valley fold the sides in while petal folding the top and bottom.

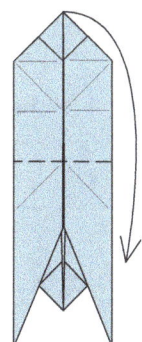
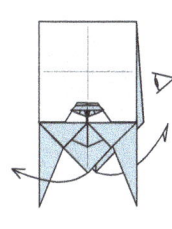

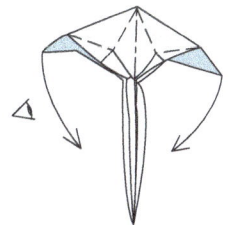

72. Valley fold down.

73. Raise the sides slightly.

74. View from previous step. Spread apart the top pleat, pulling the flap down.

75. Rabbit ear the sides down.

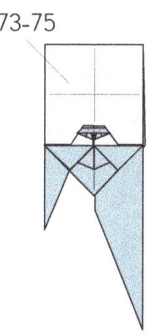
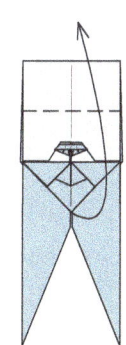
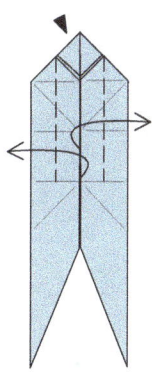
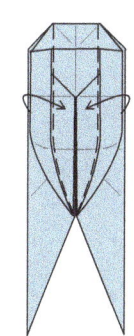

76. Repeat steps 73-75 on the other side.

77. Swing the top section up.

78. Valley fold the sides out while squashing the top corner.

79. Valley fold the sides back in.

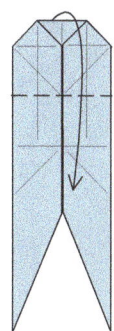
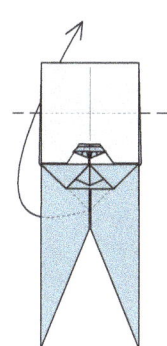
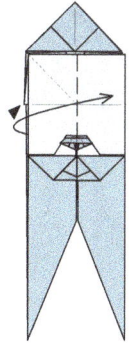
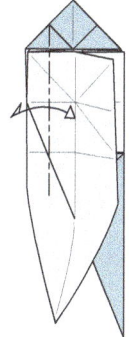

80. Valley fold down.

81. Swing the back section up.

82. Lightly valley fold over the top layer, allowing the corner to squash flat.

83. Precrease the middle layers in half with a mountain fold.

dracula

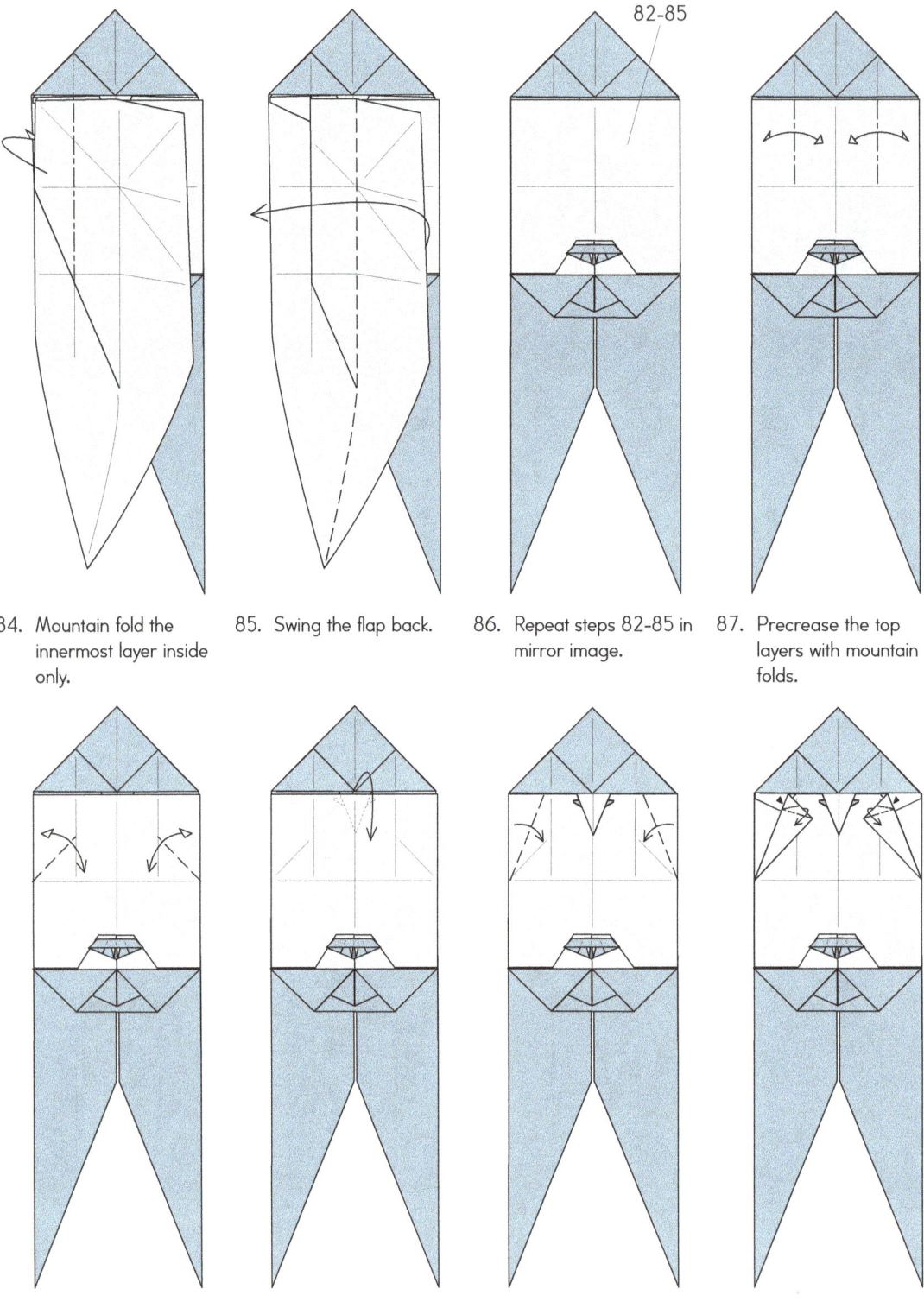

84. Mountain fold the innermost layer inside only.

85. Swing the flap back.

86. Repeat steps 82-85 in mirror image.

87. Precrease the top layers with mountain folds.

88. Precrease the top layers.

89. Bring the hidden flap to the surface.

90. Valley fold along the angle bisectors.

91. Squash the edges down.

dracula

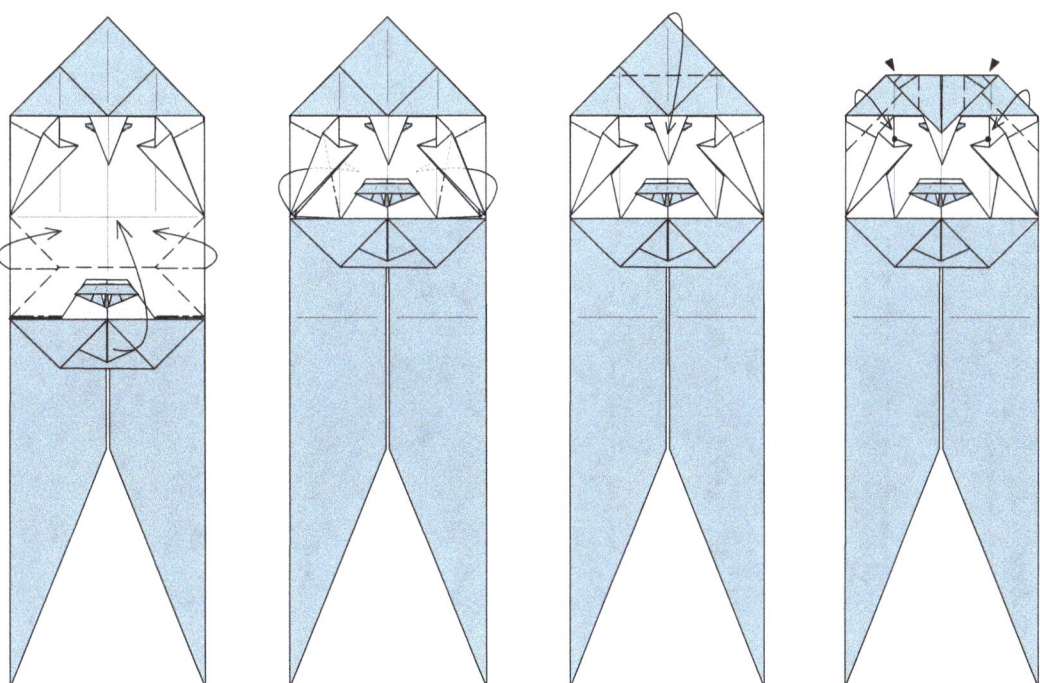

92. Pleat the flap up while reverse folding the sides.

93. Mountain fold the inner layers inside.

94. Valley fold down.

95. Valley fold to the dotted intersections, squashing at the corners.

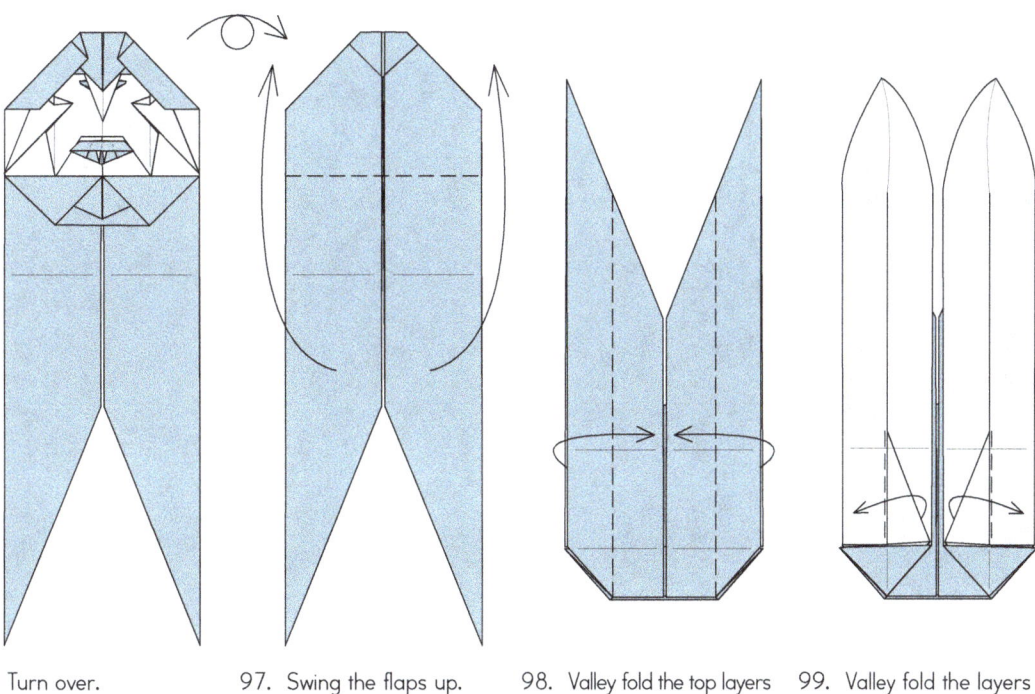

96. Turn over.

97. Swing the flaps up.

98. Valley fold the top layers to the center. The top will not lie flat.

99. Valley fold the layers outwards.

dracula

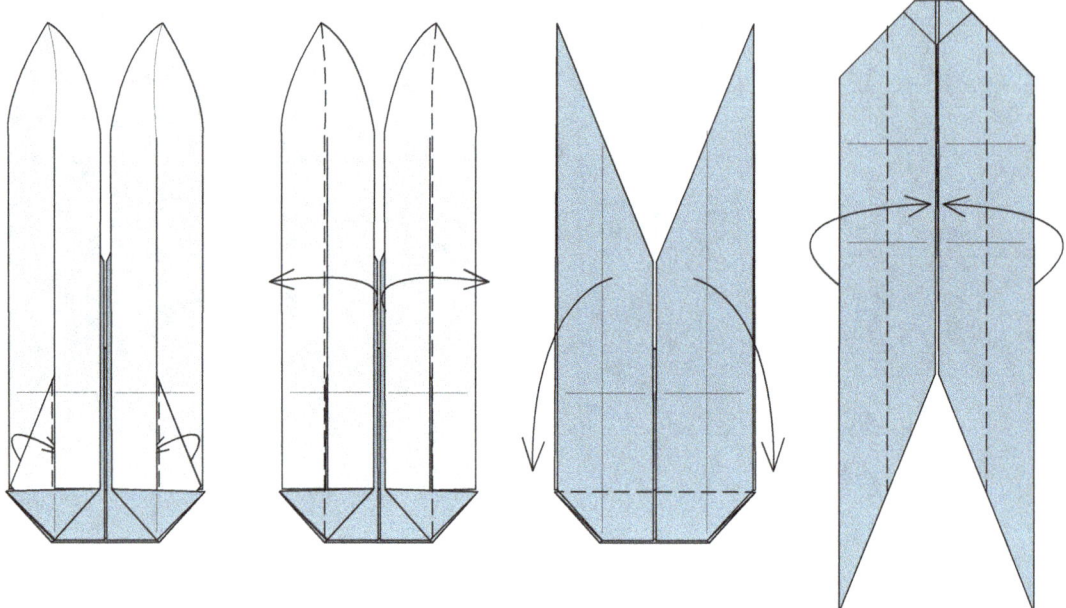

100. Valley fold the flaps inside.

101. Swing the layers outwards to flatten.

102. Swing the flaps down.

103. Valley fold the sides inwards.

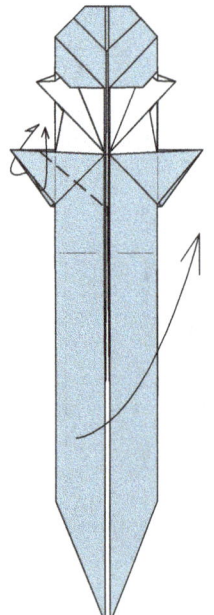

104. Outside reverse fold.

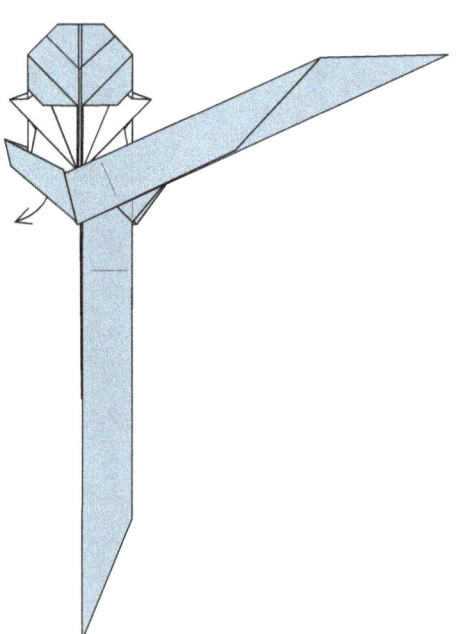

105. Pull out the trapped layer.

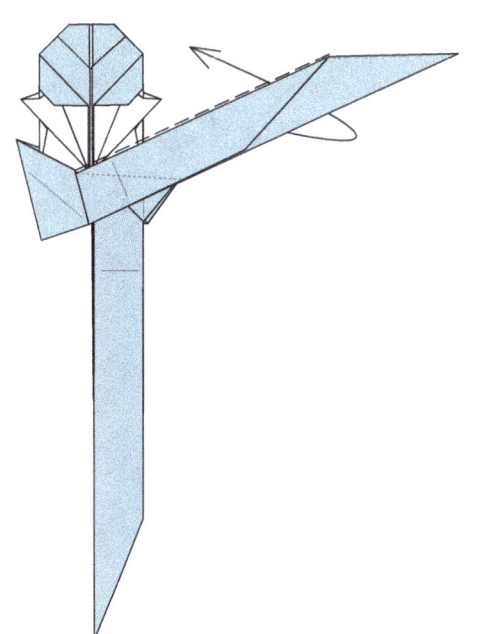
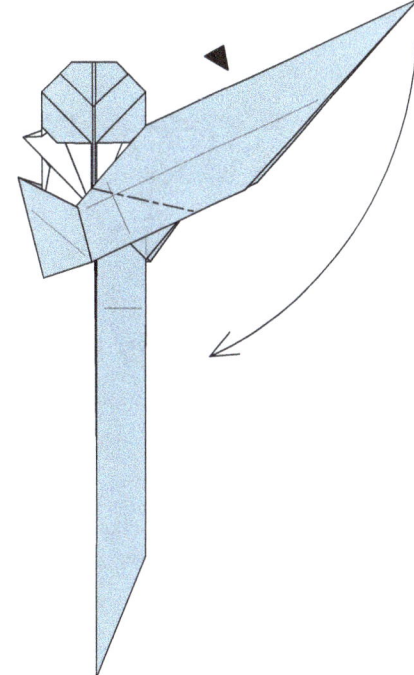

106. Raise the rear layer and flatten.

107. Squash fold the flap down towards the center, allowing it to be concave.

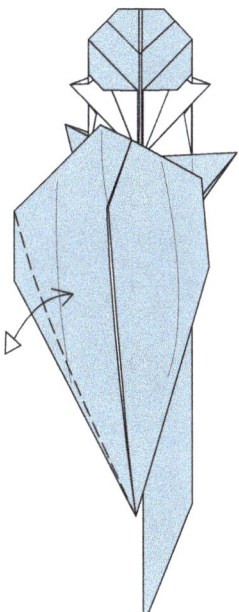
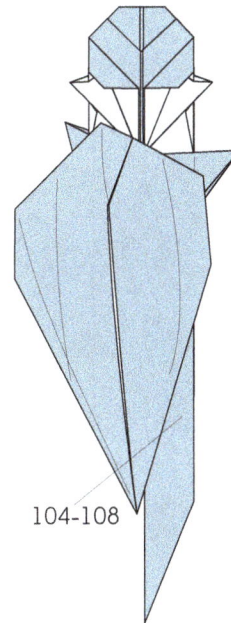
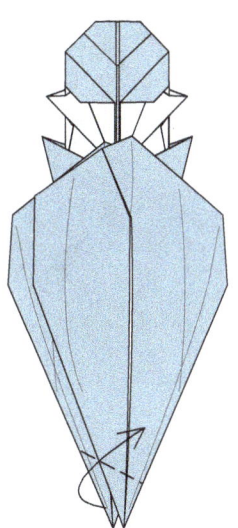
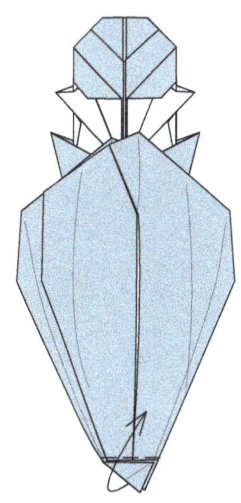

108. Precrease from corner to corner.

109. Repeat steps 104-108 in mirror image.

110. Valley fold the corners together.

111. Valley fold up.

dracula

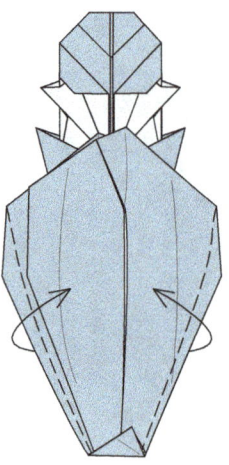

112. Valley fold the edges in along the existing creases.

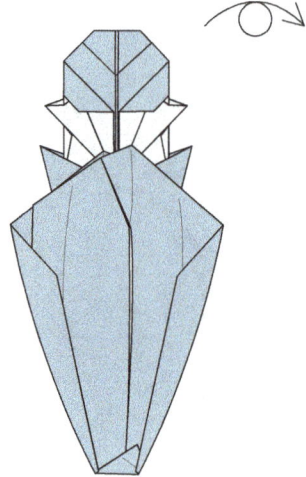

113. Turn over.

114. Completed *Dracula*.

Skeleton

As we decompose after death, only our skeletal frame remains. In folklore and modern mythologies our bones have become symbolic of the undead, with their disembodied outlines looking creepy when animated. They are closely linked to Halloween and Mexico's Day of the Dead, both of which commemorate the transitioning of spirits. This origami *Skeleton* utilizes the box-pleating style of origami master Neal Elias.

skeleton

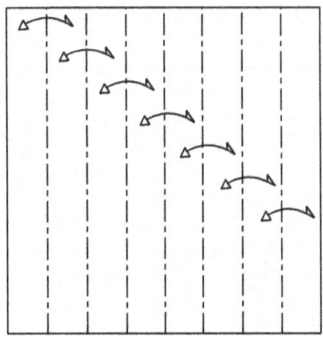

1. Precrease with mountain folds into eights.

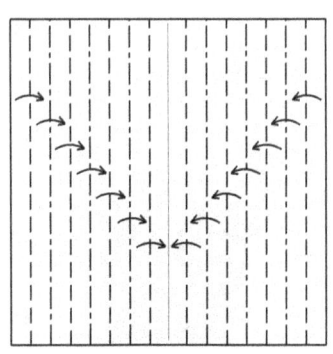

2. Insert valley folds between the creases, so as to pleat the sides towards the center.

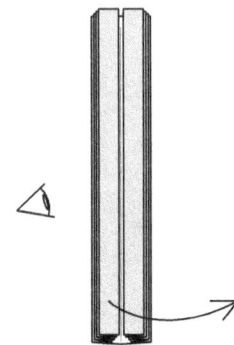

3. Spread apart one set of pleats.

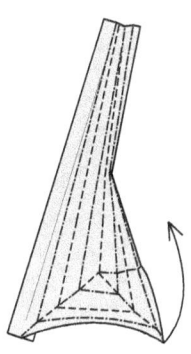

4. Stretch the corner, while pleating the bottom edge up.

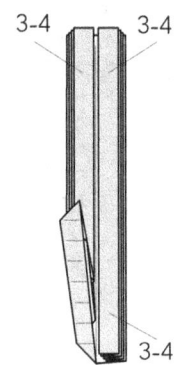

5. Repeat steps 3-4 on the other three corners.

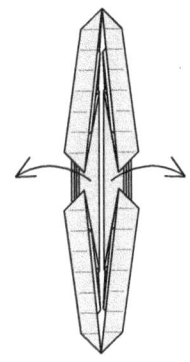

6. Unfold the model completely.

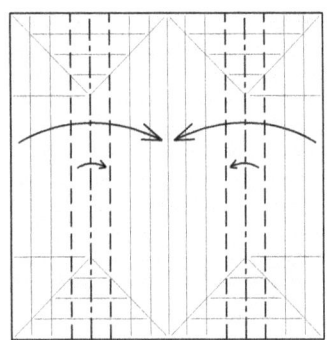

7. Valley fold the sides inwards, while inserting a pleat at each side.

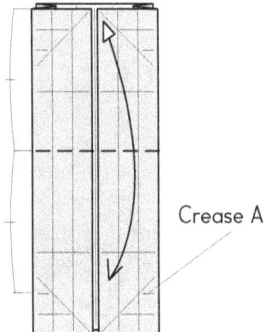

8. Precrease the top down to hit crease A.

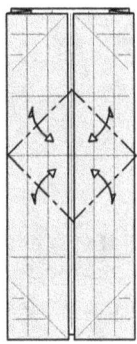

9. Precrease with mountain folds (through all layers).

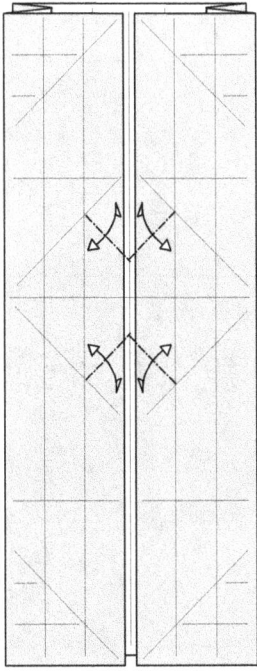

10. Precrease with mountain folds (through all layers).

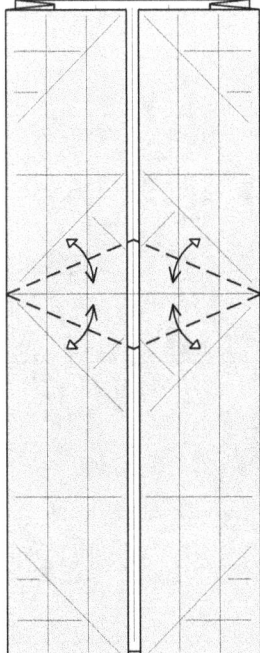

11. Precrease along the angle bisectors (through all layers).

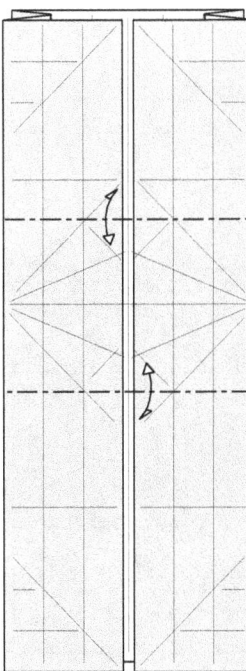

12. Precrease with mountain folds (through all layers).

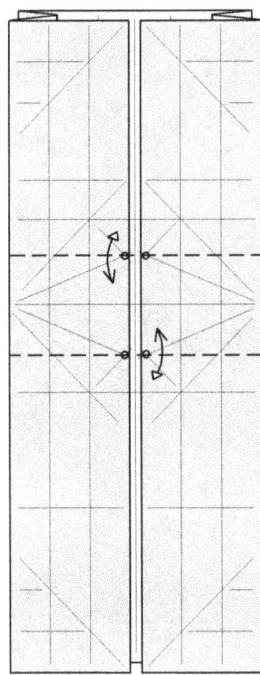

13. Precrease again (through all layers), noting the intersection of creases.

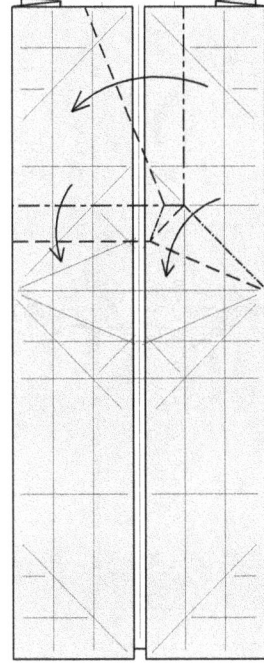

14. Form two pleats simultaneously, allowing the middle portion to collapse naturally.

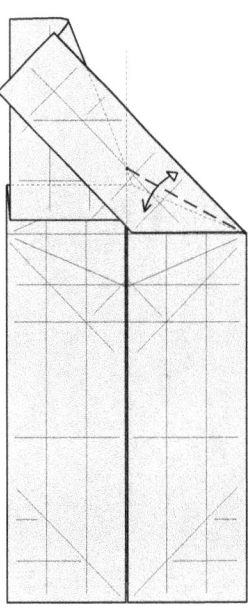

15. Precrease, using the hidden folded edges from the back as a guide.

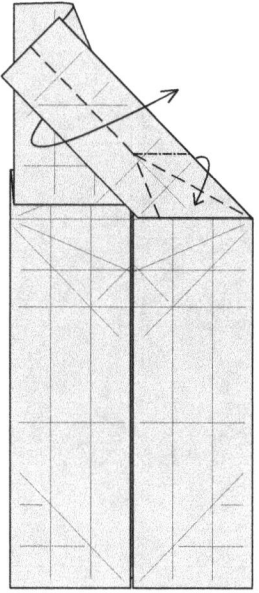

16. Swivel fold over.

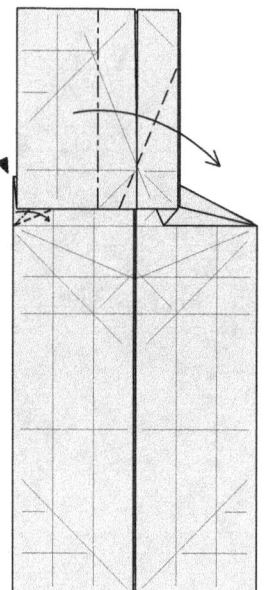

17. Squash fold (similar to step 14).

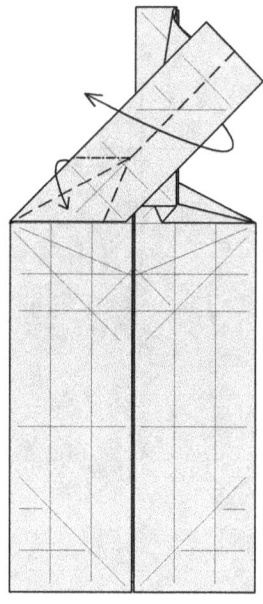

18. Swivel fold over to match the other side.

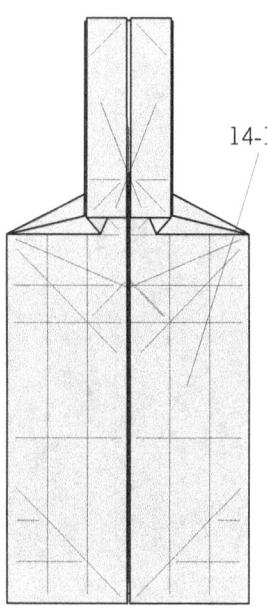

14-18

19. Repeat steps 14-18 on the bottom.

20. Turn over.

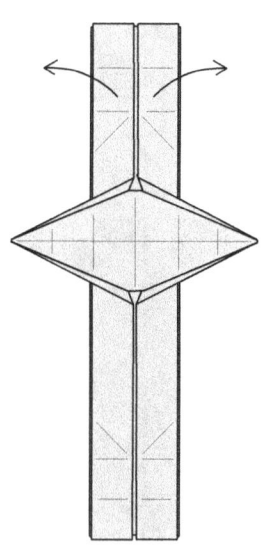

21. Unfold the top section.

skeleton

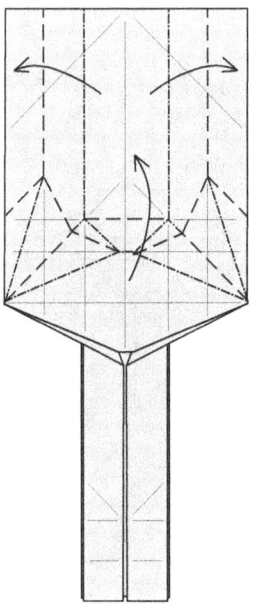

22. Collapse back as before, but reverse the direction of some of the folds on the top single layer.

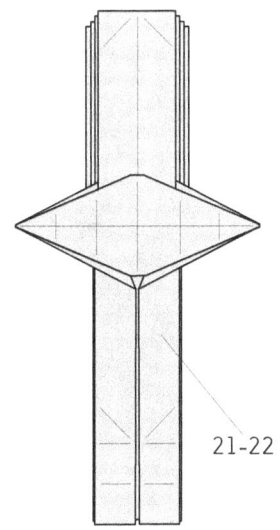

23. Repeat steps 21-22 on the bottom.

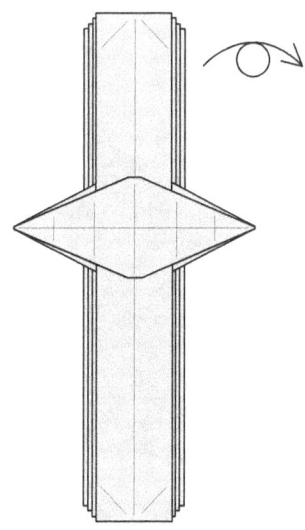

24. Turn over.

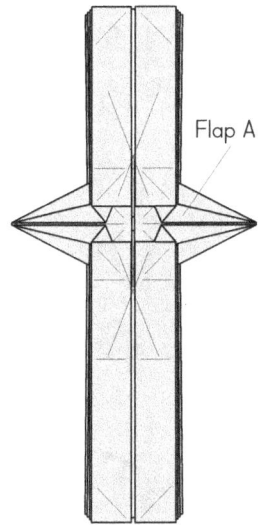

25. Note that flap A has some layers trapped within it. Release these layers from inside, and repeat on the three remaining similar flaps.

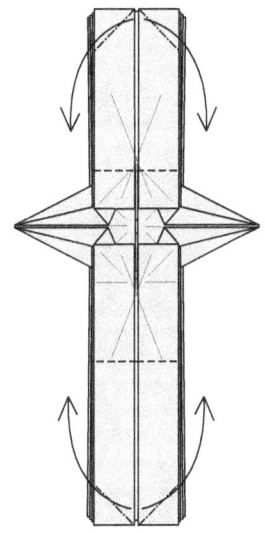

26. Stretch the four corners down, replacing the folds from steps 3-5.

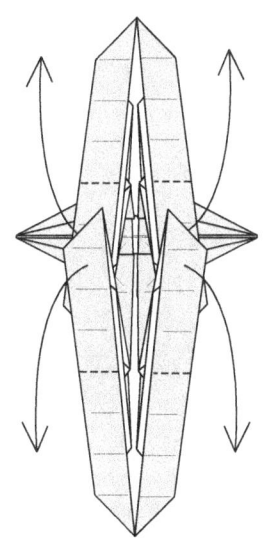

27. Fold the four points outwards.

skeleton

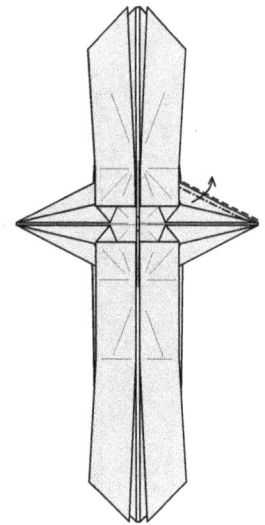

28. Swivel fold a single layer up slightly.

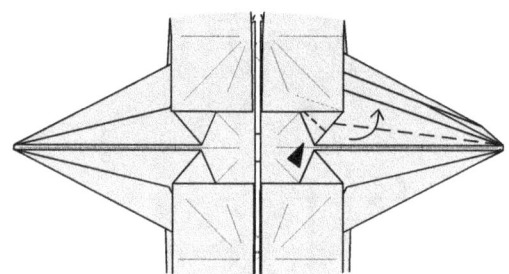

29. Reverse fold upwards along the angle bisector.

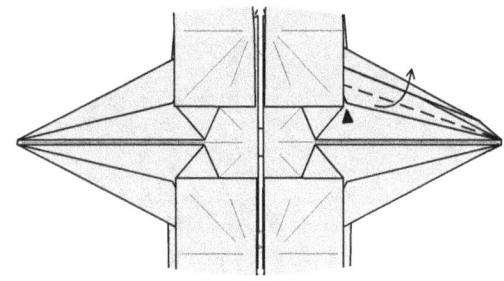

30. Reverse fold again.

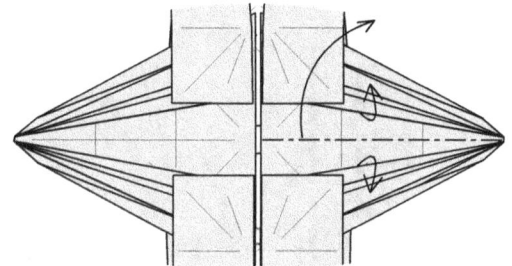

31. Reverse fold to match the flap above.

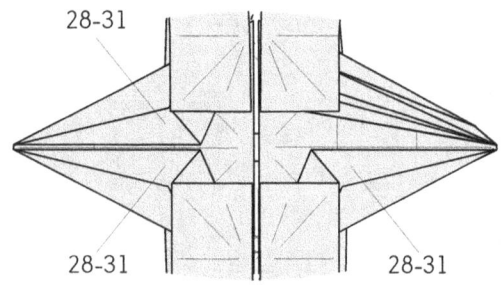

32. Repeat steps 28–31 on the other three sides.

33. Pull a single layer upwards, releasing paper from beneath the pleats. The resulting flap will not lie entirely flat.

skeleton

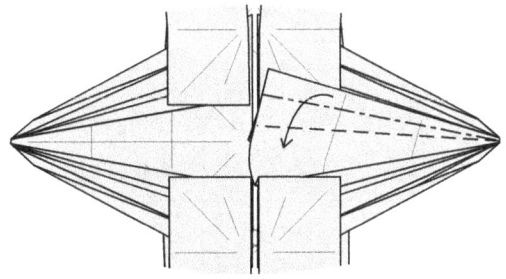

34. Pleat the flap to lie flat, and match the neighboring flaps.

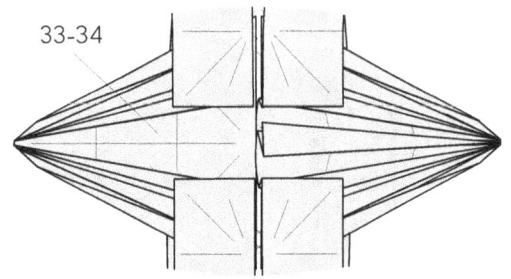

35. Repeat steps 33-34 on the other side.

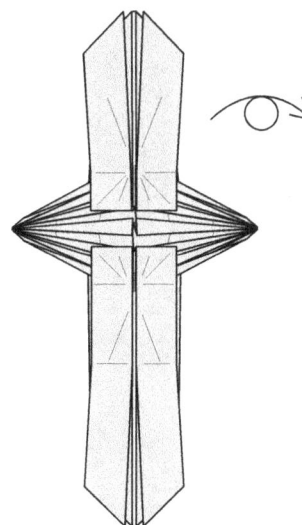

36. Turn over.

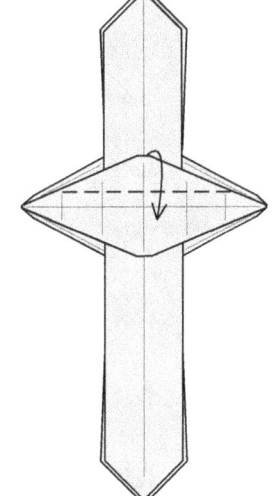

37. Valley fold down as far as possible.

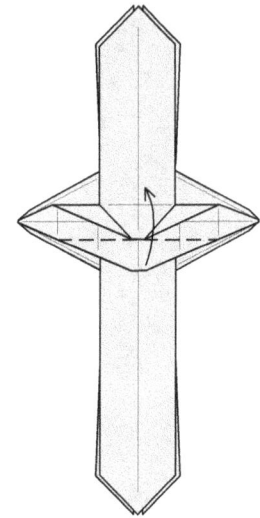

38. Valley fold up as far as possible.

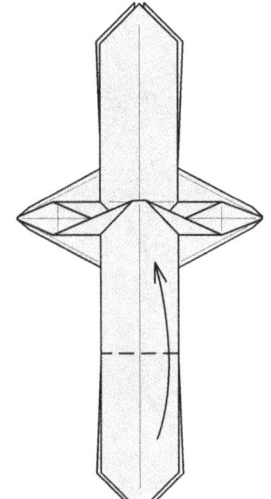

39. Valley fold up as far as possible.

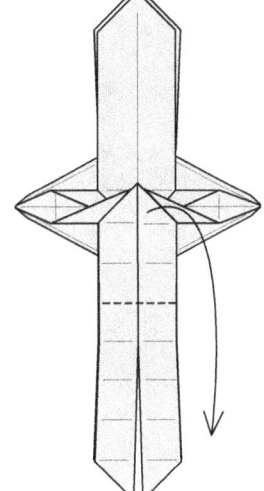

40. Valley fold down.

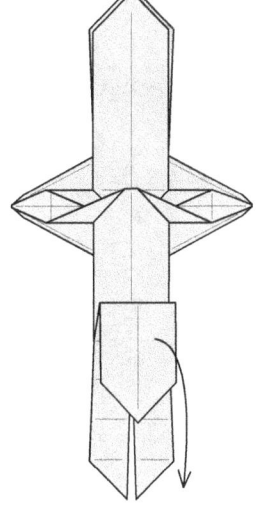

41. Open out the pleat.

skeleton

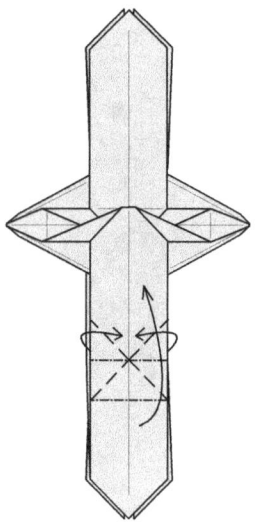

42. Replace the pleat, while incorporating reverse folds on the top layer.

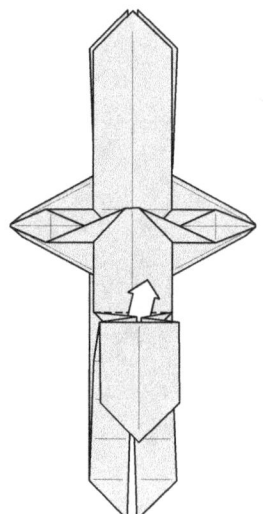

43. Unsink a single layer.

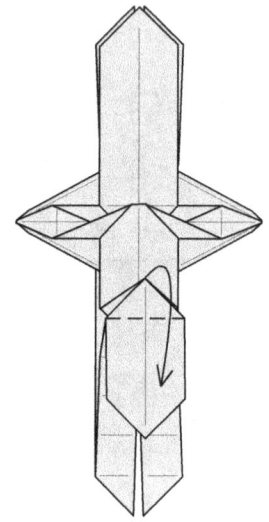

44. Valley fold down.

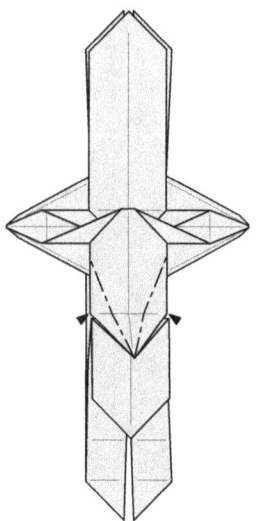

45. Sink along the angle bisectors (precrease first).

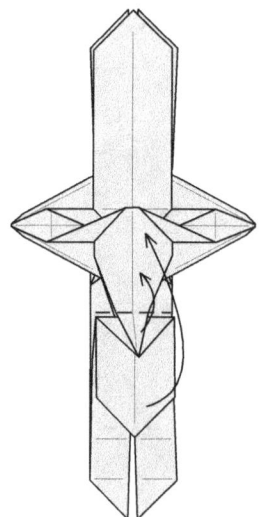

46. Swing two flaps up.

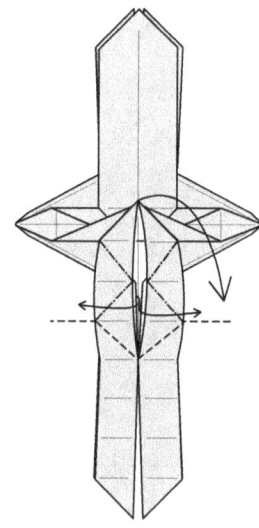

47. Swivel fold the two sets of side layers outwards, while collapsing down.

skeleton

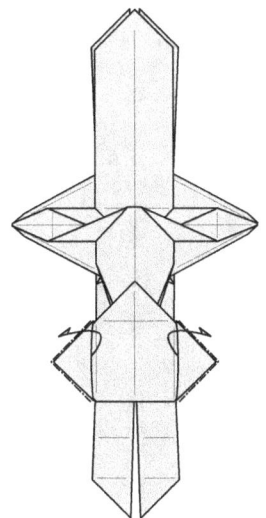

48. Wrap around the layers.

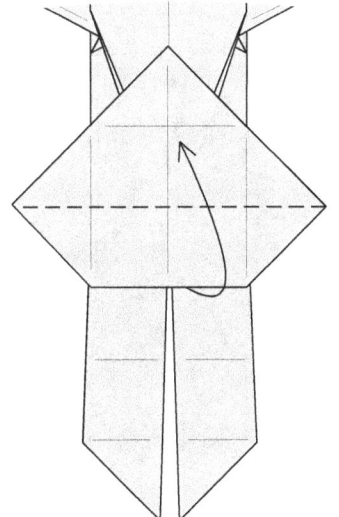

49. Valley fold up.

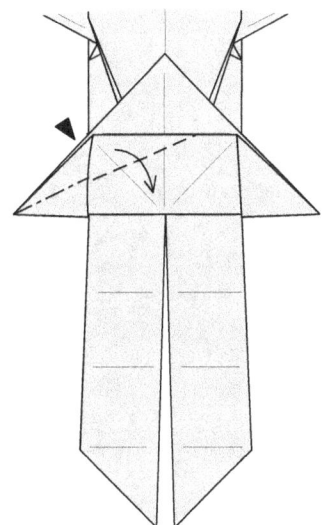

50. Squash fold.

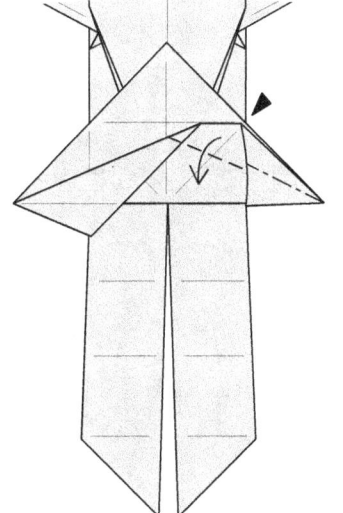

51. Squash fold again.

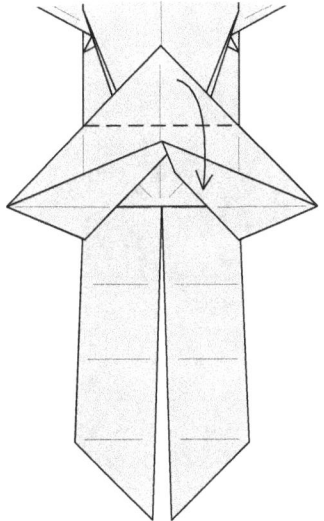

52. Swing down.

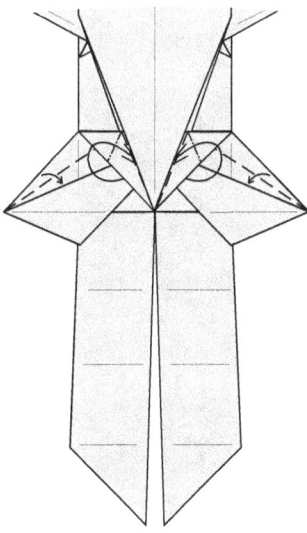

53. Swivel fold into the lower pockets on the center flap.

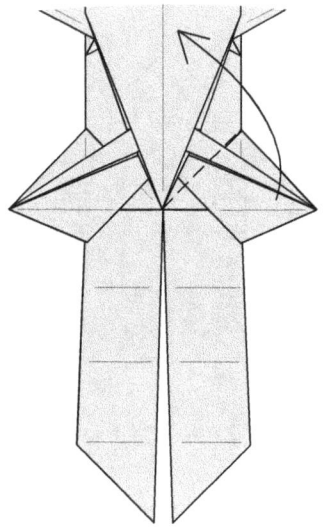  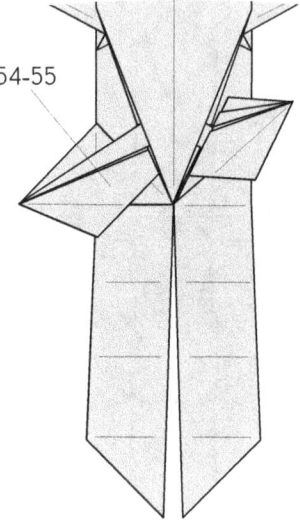

54. Valley fold up as far as possible.

55. Valley fold down, to lie against the center flap.

56. Repeat steps 54-55 on the other side.

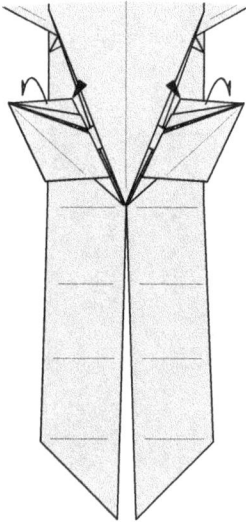  

57. Reverse fold the sides as far as possible.

58. Pull out a layer from each side.

59. Round the corners with mountain folds.

skeleton

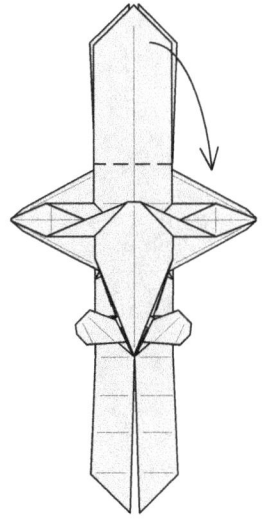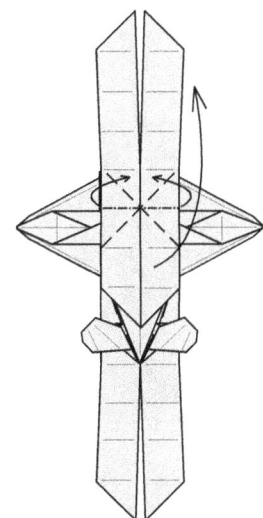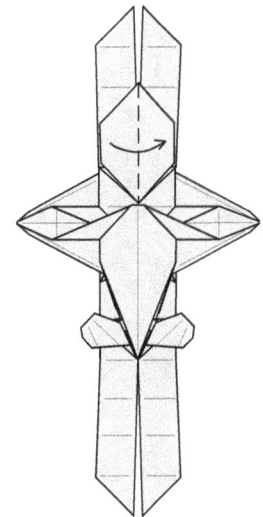

60. Valley fold down as far as possible.

61. Bring the flap up, while incorporating reverse folds on the sides.

62. Swing over.

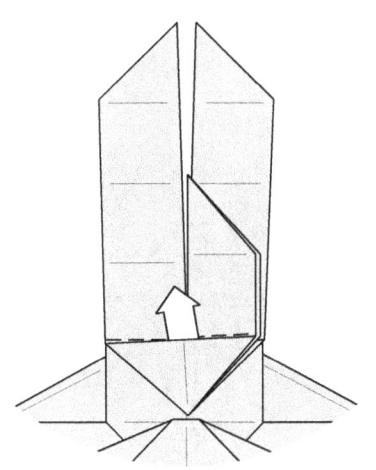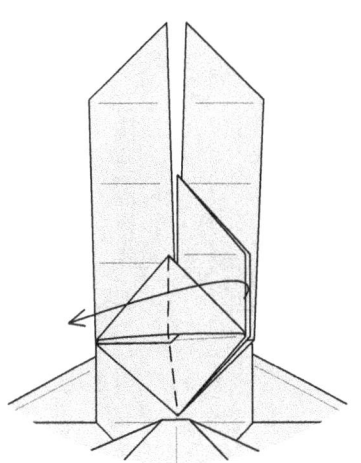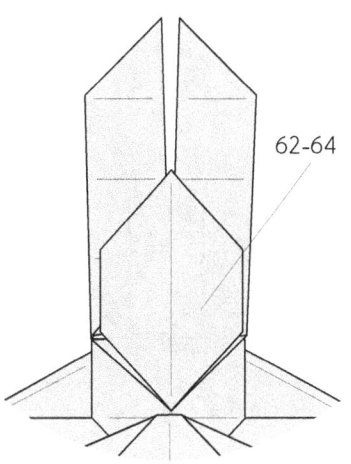

63. Pull out all of the interior layers and flatten.

64. Swing back.

65. Repeat steps 62-64 in mirror image.

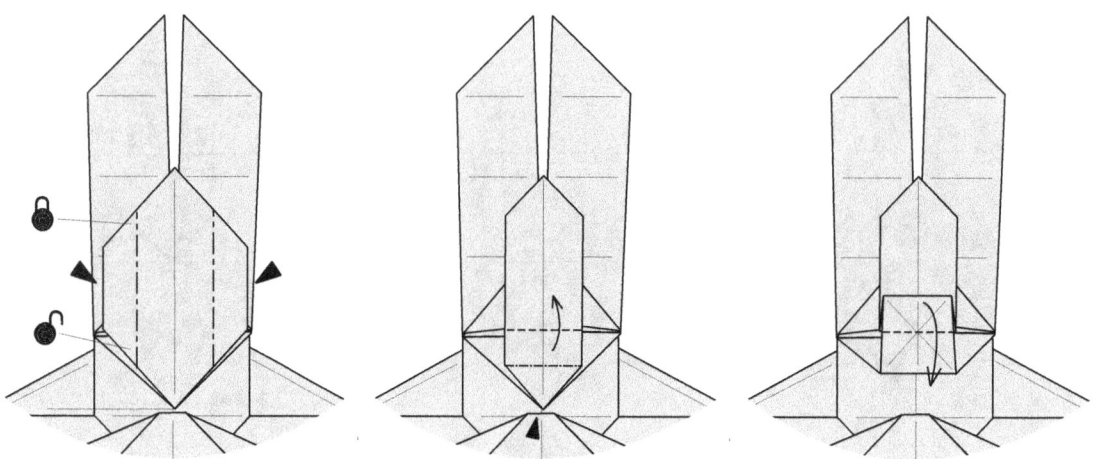

66. Sink the two sides in triangularly (closed at the top and open at the bottom).

67. Spread squash upwards. Do not flatten completely.

68. Swing the small flap down.

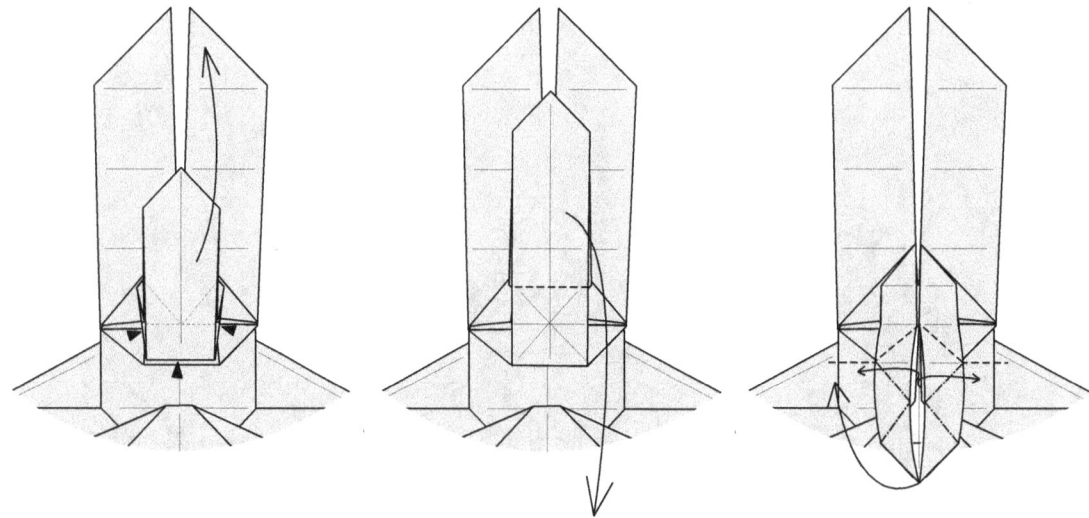

69. Stretch the flap upwards, while allowing the hidden side layers to collapse inwards.

70. Swing down.

71. Swivel the two sets of side layers outwards, while collapsing down.

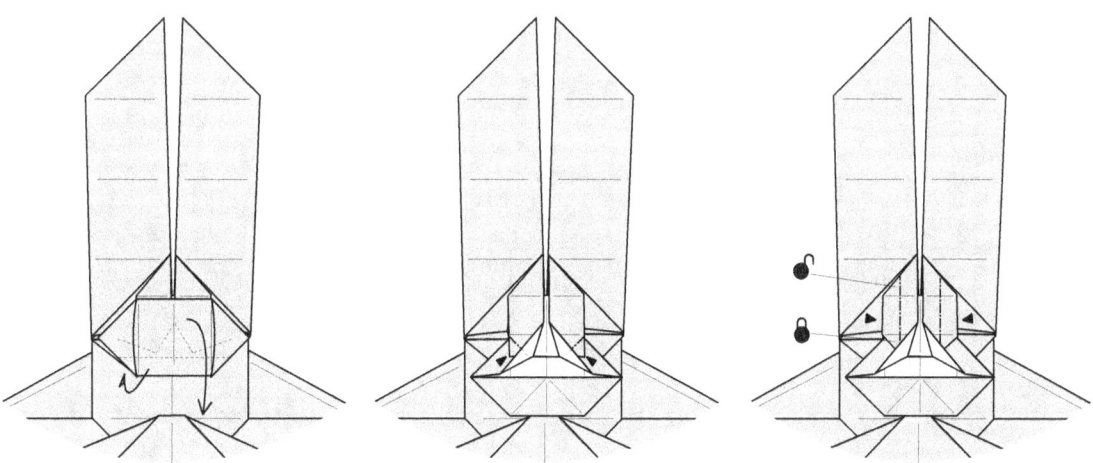

72. Flip down, allowing two squashes to form.

73. Make two reverse folds.

74. Sink the two sides in triangularly (open at the top and closed at the bottom).

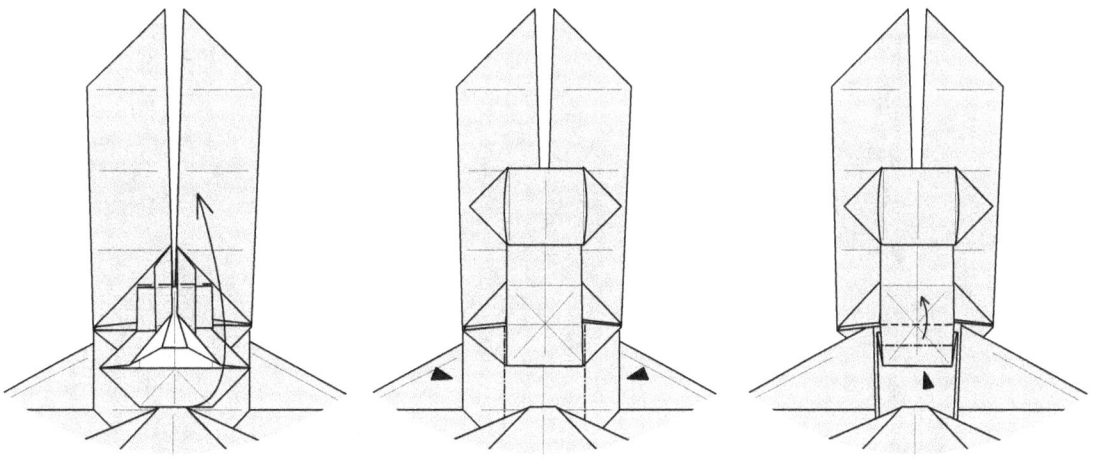

75. Swing back up.

76. Sink the sides.

77. Spread squash.

skeleton

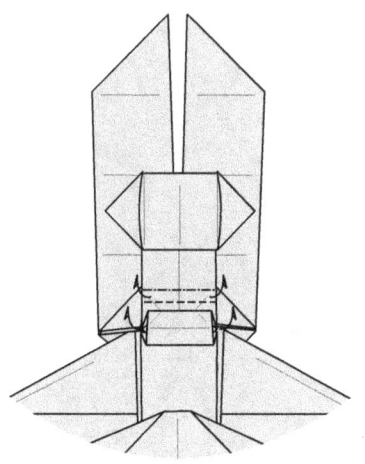 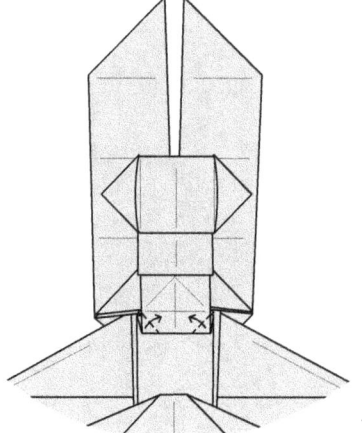 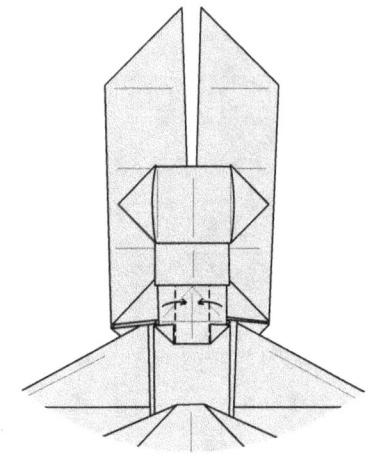

78. Pinch a pleat at the top, pulling the paper out from the pleat below.

79. Valley fold the corners.

80. Swivel fold the sides to the center.

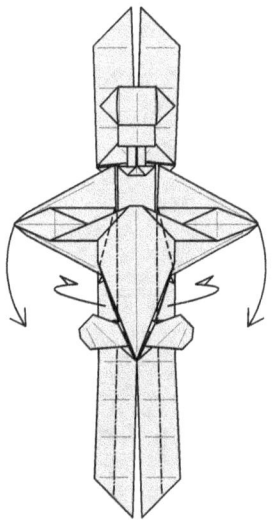 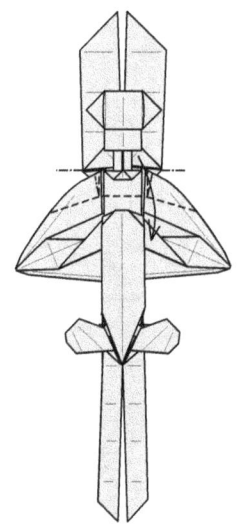 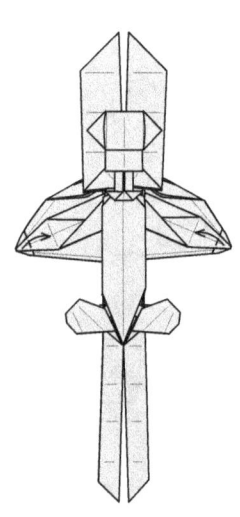

81. Mountain fold the sides in half, forming a small pleat where the ribs meet the spine. The top of the ribs will be slightly concave.

82. Pleat the top section down, allowing two small pleats to form. Do not fold too sharply.

83. Valley fold in the tips.

skeleton

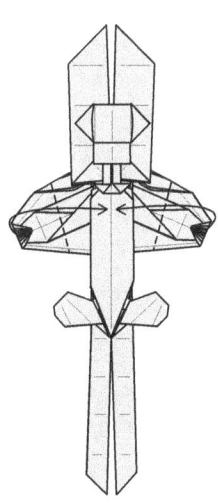
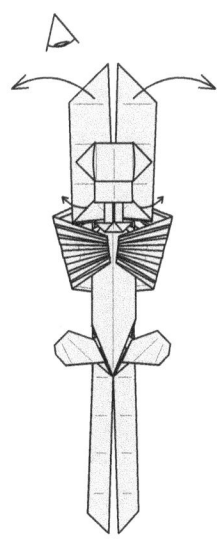
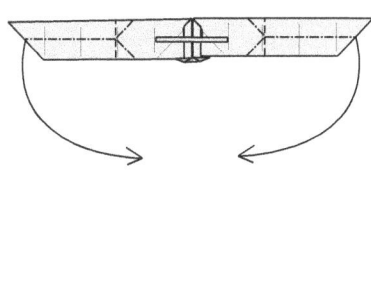

84. Lightly valley fold the sides towards the center.

85. Pull out the arms out at 90° angles, releasing the trapped paper. The back will not lie flat.

86. View from step 85. Rabbit ear the arms downwards at 90° angles.

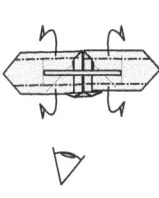
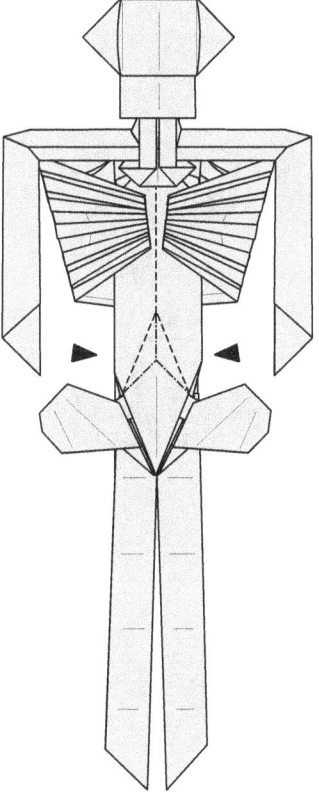
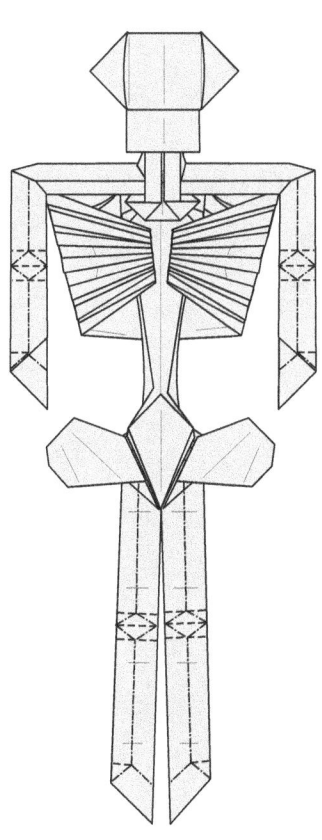

87. Mountain fold the sides down at 90° angles.

88. Pinch the sides inward, forming a rabbit ear at the base.

89. Thin the legs and arms, inserting rabbit ears where indicated.

109

skeleton

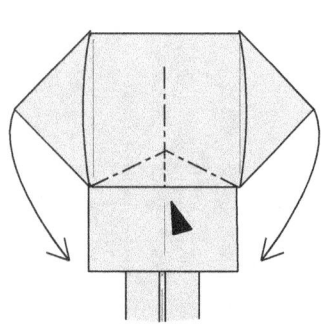 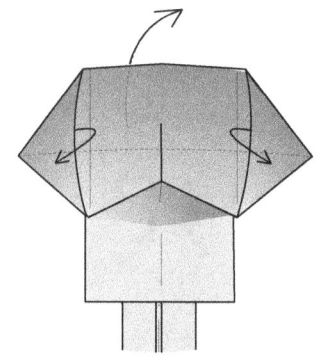 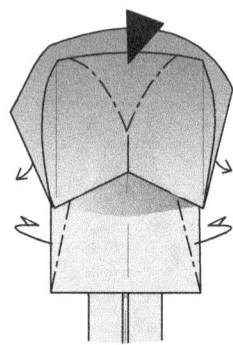

90. Make the nose 3-D, while pulling down the sides.

91. Open out the eye sockets, while pulling out the single layer from the back.

92. Add additional shaping to the head and the rest of the model to taste.

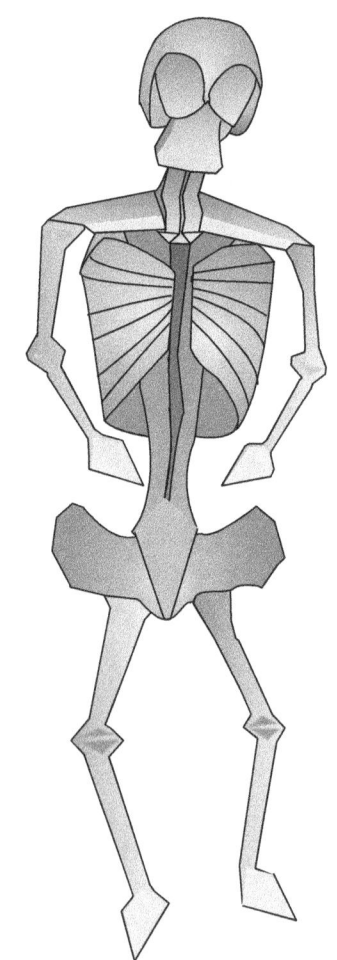

93. Completed *Skeleton*.

Materials and Methods

In theory, the only things required for origami is a piece of paper and a pair of hands. In practice, however, you will want to have the right materials for the project at hand. For initial practice attempts, you will want to use papers that are easy to fold, but not necessarily of presentable quality. The two most popular practice papers are commercial origami paper (sometimes sold as kami) and American foil. Both papers are available colored on one side, and white on the other. American foil is preferable as it holds its shape more easily. These papers feature a thin layer of decorative foil that helps your model hold its shape. Most of the origami supply houses sell a 10" version as their largest size, but some thinner wrapping paper can be used if you are looking for something larger. Japanese foil is thinner, and generally easier to fold than the American variety, albeit more expensive. Kami is better for those who have trouble with reverse folds and sinks. Both types of papers will yield adequate results, but almost invariably, more decorative choices will make your models look better.

For display-worthy efforts, you will want to use papers and methods that heighten the result, possibly at the expense of ease of folding. Such methods include foil-backing and wet folding, which includes the related technique of back coating. Both approaches allow the paper-folding artist to use material combinations to create interesting effects.

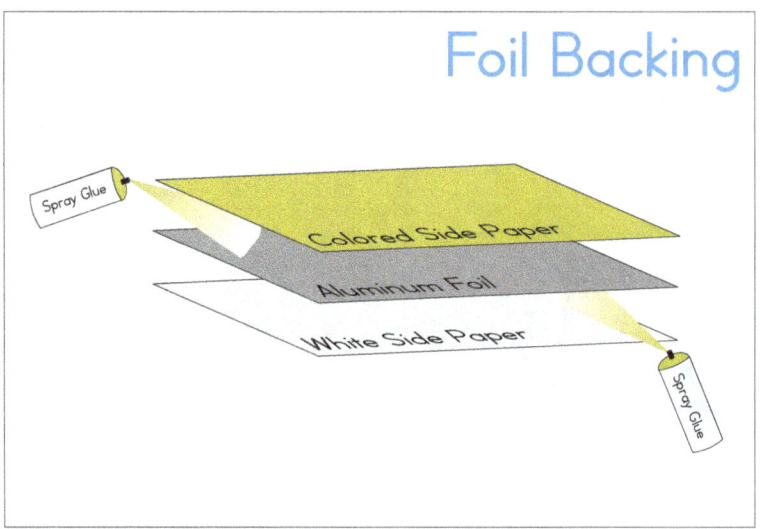

Foil Backing

Foil backing is a great way to utilize nonporous materials, and papers with patterns that could get ruined with water (such as newsprint). Foil backing is the process of adding a layer of aluminum foil (yes, the same material you can find at virtually any grocery store) to paper, to give the resulting material unique folding characteristics. A common backing choice is tissue paper, which further enhances the folding properties of the foil (this combination is also known as "tissue foil"). Regardless of the backing material, the metal-like quality allows folds to instantly stay where they are placed. Spray adhesive is used to bond the layers together. This is also known as artist's adhesive or photo mounting spray, and it contains the same glue found on adhesive tape. You can find this at most art supply stores, but you will find it much cheaper at a hardware or office supply store. While you can usually use 3M's Spray Mount, some projects (typically involving very thick papers) will require something like 3M's Super77 Spray Adhesive. All work should be done in a well-ventilated area, as the glue is toxic. You will also want to protect your floor with newspaper. Place a sheet of foil on the floor. Leave the shinier side up first and use as the surface for the main color. In most cases, the foil will be the limiting factor as far as size is concerned, so use as large a sheet as necessary. Spray the glue onto the surface of the foil according to the manufacturer's directions.

If you have a choice of nozzles, use the one with a finer mist. When spraying, be sure to cover the entire surface area of the foil, while paying special attention to the edges. After spraying, you should give the glue about a minute to get tacky.

The next step is to apply your paper to the tacky surface. Start by adhering the bottom edge of your paper to the bottom edge of the foil. Then start working your way upwards until the foil is completely covered. You can also use a baker's rolling pin to apply the paper. Another variation is to start at one corner and work your way to the opposite corner. Try several methods to see which feels most comfortable. For thicker papers, it might be easier to simply drop the paper onto the foil. When you are done, rub out any wrinkles, and then apply another layer of paper on the other side.

To get the largest possible square, cut along the edge of the foil, which should be visible through the layers of paper, provided your papers are translucent enough. If you wish you can also tear through the foil, which is surprisingly accurate (and fun), provided you are using thin enough paper. First, score the paper, unfold, and turn over to leave the resulting crease in mountain fold formation. The paper can easily be torn in this position. Of course, you won't get the largest possible square this way, but it is easier to be accurate.

A rotary cutting board is recommended when tearing is not possible, or you cannot see the silhouette of the foil through your backing paper. While a traditional guillotine cutter might suffice, spending an extra $100 or so on a rotary cutter is worth the investment for the serious paperfolding artist. These can be purchased at better art supply stores or photography supply stores. A pair of scissors can be used when a paper cutter is not as convenient.

If you wish to make a square that is wider than your piece of foil, there is a way to accomplish this. First, you must adhere two (or more) strips of foil together. If you spray along the edge of one piece and attach the other piece along that edge, the results are remarkably seamless. Most likely, the paper you will want to use on the surface will be smaller than the foil piece you have prepared. There is a way around this hurdle as well. First, you should fold your foil in half. The resulting surface area should now be small enough for your paper. Before you use any adhesive, place a sheet of newspaper between the fold to avoid getting any glue on the inner layers. You can now adhere your papers on each side of the foil. When you are done with the gluing part, use a scissor to cut along the folded edge. After you unfold your piece, rub out the crease, and the seam will almost disappear. You can repeat the same process for the other side.

When folding larger models, you might find certain portions to be flimsy. While wire is traditionally used to add rigidity, I have found stuffing layers of foil to be even better. You can fold a piece of foil over upon itself a few times to make it many layers thick. This can be stuffed between the layers of the parts of the model that need more rigidity.

If you are using tissue as the backing paper, where the properties of the foil are at their most extreme, you are in for a radically different folding experience. By themselves, foil and tissue make for flimsy and weak folding materials, but together you have one of the strongest and most resilient materials around. Also, when you make a crease, it will hold very well. It will hold so well that it is difficult to change its direction (i.e., valley to mountain). This makes procedures that require precreasing, such as sinks, difficult to perform. You can unfold the paper after precreasing, rub out the creases must be changed, and replace them with new folds that are in the right direction. Unlike commercial foil paper, you can rub out unwanted creases without leaving a trace.

While it is true that foil backing will make folding your model more difficult for most if its stages, its properties are fortuitous at the end of a model's folding sequence. If your model has many layers, it can easily be flattened. In extreme cases, a hammer can work wonders. After your model is as flat as you desire, you can shape and pose it any way you wish. Your model will hold that shape forever, until you decide to reshape it, or someone or something inadvertently reshapes it. The latter scenario is obviously undesirable. If you use a slightly thicker paper (such as the Japanese papers), you will lose some of the malleability but will have a much more solid looking model, due to its increased thickness. It can still be bent out of shape, but is acceptable if being displayed in a controlled environment.

Wet Folding

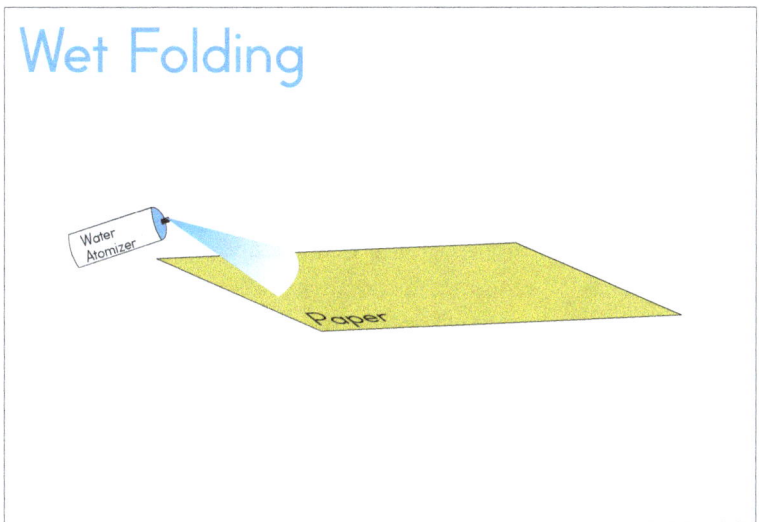

Foil backed paper looks great in person, but the camera lens often picks up the foil through the backing, even when the backing paper seems to be dense enough. This might be okay for some subjects, but to have a less reflective look, wet folding techniques are more effective. The process might be slower, but the results are more permanent.

Wet folding involves lightly dampening your paper during the folding process, so when it finally dries it will retain its shape. When paper is wet, the sizing (glue-like substance) that holds the paper fibers together is loosened. Once the paper is dry again, the sizing will hold the paper in its new position. Taking advantage of this property of paper enables the folder to hold shapes that seem to defy gravity. Not all papers contain a lot of sizing, so you might have to add a methylcellulose paste to your paper before folding. To do this, you first add the methylcellulose powder (which is sold at many art supply stores) to water and mix the compound until it is syrupy. You can use about a teaspoon for each cup of warm water. This paste can now be brushed onto your paper with a standard painter's brush. After the paper is dry, it will be even easier to wet fold. To speed up the drying process, you can use a table fan.

When wet folding it is important to realize your paper will expand, often unevenly. This makes accurate folding much more difficult. Also, reference fold crease lines become difficult to see while paper is wet. For these reasons, you may prefer to delay wetting the paper until key folds are in place. When you are ready to wet the paper, it is important not to allow the paper to get soggy. By using an atomizer's mist sparingly, a leathery texture can be obtained from the paper. These spray bottles can be found at many perfume sections; try to find one with as fine a mist as possible.

Holding your model in position while drying can be a creative challenge. Tools that work include twist ties (the plastic-coated ones that are often used for electrical wire packing), portable clamps, and painter's masking tape. As an example, you can wind a twist tie around the legs of your insect model, bend them into the desired position, and secure them to a flat surface with masking tape. After further moistening your model with your atomizer, it will retain its stance after it is dry and the bindings have been removed.

Back Coating

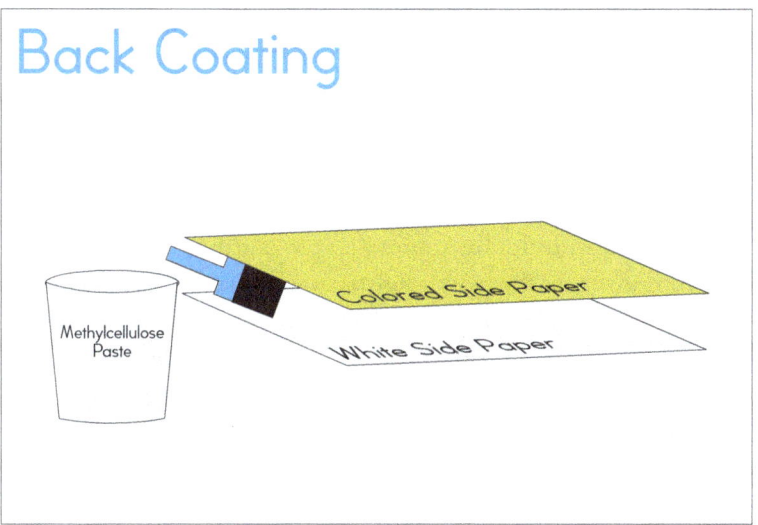

A related technique to wet folding is back coating. Since most specialty papers are monochromatic, the two-toned effect in many origami models is lost. You can use methylcellulose paste to adhere two complementing colors of paper together. Brush the paste on one paper, being sure to work on a smooth surface, as the paper will pick up any texture from your working surface. Apply the second sheet on top, brushing it into place. You can cut your square once it is dry, using a table fan to expedite the process. Again, a rotary cutter is recommended. The materials you chose to mate together should both be porous and fibrous enough to stay together, otherwise you might have to resort to foil backing.

Papers that work well include the Unryu variety (both regular and soft) from both Japan and Thailand. These papers might be labeled as containing mulberry or kozo fiber, but other fibers will work as well. You can also try Yatsuo papers from Japan, which are made from kozo and sulfite pulp, and have a much smoother look than the Unryu papers. These and other fine art papers can be found at better art stores and via mail order. You can expect to pay about three to four dollars for a 25" x 37" sheet.

Other important paper considerations include weight, which is how a material's thickness is described. To give you a gauge of what this means, standard copy paper is often at 20 Gr/M2 weight. Of course, you will double your thickness if you are bonding two sheets together. Try to keep the total thickness under 80 Gr/M2. When dealing with lighter colors, you might have to work with thicker papers just to get the right opacity (but you can mate them with lighter weight darker papers if you are trying to avoid additional thickness). As a test, you can hold the paper against a black surface to see how well it eclipses its backing. Sometimes, having the contrasting color show through is a good thing, as your color choices will seem to blend a bit. One thing you would like to avoid is having your paper bleed (having the dye run) when wet. The most temperamental colors tend to be reds and black, but it is a good idea to test out a sheet first if possible.

Dry Wiring

Both wet folding and foil backing will give your models a sculpted look. Sometimes is preferable to have a crisper look, where the paper looks less molded and more folded. Simply folding your paper without any of these special techniques will sometimes work, but for most models (especially those that are very complex), will have sections that will gradually spring apart. The solution is to strategically add wire to these troublesome sections.

For most models, florists wire will suffice. 26 gauge is a good thickness for most scenarios, and 22 gauge can be used where more strength is needed (lower numbers correlate with thicker gauges). The wire typically has a PVC coating (often green) that can be secured simply with a few pieces of scotch tape. For some heavier duty situations, PVC glue is useful. It can be cut with a pair scissors, but heavier gauges might be best trimmed with a wire cutter.

The wire has a palpable thickness, and it can sometimes be a challenge to avoid having it bulge through the surface layers of your model. It is best to lay the wire along a fold line that is on the underside of your model. In rare cases, you can cover the wire with multiple layers of aluminum foil to cover up the bulge.

It will be necessary to unfold and refold your model, adding wire as you feel it is helpful. Of course, this adds to the challenge of folding, but when done well, the results are worth it. As with foil backing, the final model can get bent out of shape, so special care is needed when storing. With enough experimentation, you should be able to conceive the perfect material for any model.

Paper Sizes

Skull with Bow
6 in / 15 cm
or larger

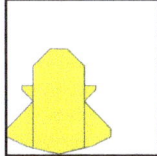
Ghost
6 in / 15 cm
or larger

Black Cat
6 in / 15 cm
or larger

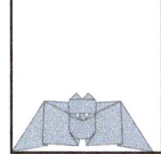
Bat
6 in / 15 cm
or larger

Jack-o'-lantern
6 in / 15 cm
or larger

Spider
10 in / 25 cm
or larger

Alien
6 in / 15 cm
or larger

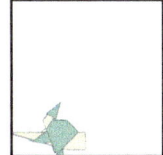
Witch
10 in / 25 cm
or larger

Grim Reaper
10 in / 25 cm
or larger

Japanese Monster
15 in / 40 cm
or larger

Hand in the Box
15 in / 40 cm
or larger

Dracula
15 in / 40 cm
or larger

Skeleton
15 in / 40 cm
or larger

www.ingramcontent.com/pod-product-compliance
Lightning Source LLC
Chambersburg PA
CBHW081751100526
44592CB00015B/2384